Dead Man Working

Dead Man Working

Carl Cederström and Peter Fleming

Winchester, UK
Washington, USA

First published by Zero Books, 2012
Zero Books is an imprint of John Hunt Publishing Ltd., Laurel House, Station Approach,
Alresford, Hants, SO24 9JH, UK
office1@o-books.net
www.o-books.com

For distributor details and how to order please visit the 'Ordering' section on our website.

Text copyright: Carl Cederström and Peter Fleming 2011

ISBN: 978 1 78099 156 6

A CIP catalogue record for this book is available from the British Library.

Design: Lee Nash

Printed and bound by CPI Group (UK) Ltd, Croydon, CR0 4YY
Printed in the USA by Offset Paperback Mfrs, Inc

We operate a distinctive and ethical publishing philosophy in all
areas of our business, from our global network of authors to
production and worldwide distribution.

CONTENTS

Dead Man Working

Even its most ardent supporters admit that capitalism died sometime in the 1970s. All attempts to resuscitate it failed. Yet strangely, now that it's dead, it's become the only game in town, more powerful and influential than ever. This book is about what it means to live and work in a dead world. A good place to begin is Franco 'Bifo' Berardi's dark YouTube lullaby 'Waiting for the Tsunami.' In vivid prose that blends poetry with theory, and acute observation with art, he draws a desolate picture of our present condition. In a dying West rife with war, mental fatigue, financial atrophy and a mania for pointless work, we find our selves adrift, overwhelmed by nothing but a sense of emptiness … and waiting. Bifo begins: *before the tsunami hits, you know how it is? The sea recedes, leaving a dead desert in which only cynicism and dejection remain.* What is truly petrifying is that something even worse is about to happen. But that is still to come. Meanwhile, we wander through this dying social architecture, slowly suffocating in a desert of extinct codes and inane loneliness. And then on the horizon, we see it. The wave! Although it is still some way off, it's close enough to make our everyday concerns look absurd and futile. In light of the wave that will surely erase your existence, the command to work, procreate, consume, relax, be happy, be ethical, to obey – in short, the command to live – can now safely be ignored. As the wave draws closer, you feel strangely at ease. No more demands. All you need to do, Bifo concludes, is to make *sure you have the right words to say, the right clothes to wear, before it finally wipes you away.*

The dark awareness that is provoked by the incoming wave is further unpacked in Bifo's *The Soul at Work*:

Breathing has become difficult, almost impossible: as a matter of fact, one suffocates. One suffocates every day, and the symptoms of suffocation are disseminated all along the paths of daily life … our chances of survival are few: we know it. There is no alternative to capitalism.

The somatic desolation described here is grounded in a kind of hyper-hopelessness, an existence more properly defined by its opposite, that of non-living, a life that is already dead. After speaking with workers in a wide range of occupations, both at the top and bottom of the social hierarchy, we will argue in this book that this feeling of non-living is no more pervasive than among the multitude of workers trapped in the modern corporation. Whether in the office, the call center, the service counter, in the creative industries, the retail show-floor or the backroom warehouse, life seems to be far away. We have always known that capitalism accumulates numerical value by subtracting social value, experienced as alienation, disenchantment and dehumanization. But what has now become evident is the sheer pointlessness of our daily endeavors. A quest without end or rationale, slowly poisoning almost every aspect of our lives on the job and even afterwards when we think the daily grind is over. But, of course, it is *never* over. In an eccentric and extreme society like ours, working has assumed a universal presence – a 'worker's society' in the worst sense of the term – where even the unemployed and children find themselves obsessed with it. This viral-like logic of the corporation has even spread into our most intimate pastimes, precipitating a novel and inescapable cultural malaise, writ-large by a complete, irreversible and ominous *dead end*.

Bifo's characterization of the living dead paralyzed before the wave is a telling reading of how we experience capitalism today. Most despise it for what it has made us become; yet we have no imaginative energy left to look beyond it. But this bleak parable does miss something important if we are to truly understand the mindset of the dead man working. In Bifo's rendition, the metaphor of the incoming wave functions well only until the last instant, when it finally does arrive and wipe us away. Unfortunately our predicament is worse. What if that last instant never comes? *What if the wave never arrives to end our misery?* Perhaps this is the real tragedy underlining the dead man working. Even the hope of non-existence is snatched from us as we are hemmed into a manufactured dead end. We work *as if* we are about to die, *as if* we are about to be unburdened from the deadweight of work, but we never actually are until it is too late. Unlike past generations of workers who were told they either work or die on the scrapheap, it is not death that terrifies us today. We would welcome some terminus to relieve us from this living hell. No, what frightens us more than dying is the thought of *not dying*, being wedded to a life that is not worth living.

Perhaps this is the trouble with so many apocalyptic accounts of Western capitalism today, from Slavoj Žižek's compelling *Living in the End Times* to the strange popularity of the 'end-of the-world' film *Battle LA* (which was also voted by many the worst movie of 2011). The expectation of some kind of end or conclusion may inadvertently feed into a seductive ideological distortion: the fantasy of release and escape. A fantasy that we might, for better or worse, someday be finished with all of this. The ideology of exit conceals, however, a mood that is now pervading large parts of our society. Yes, it is unbearable, but also, and *paradoxically*, unending. The Beckettian stuck-in-a-rut joke …

Estragon: I can't go on like this.
Vladimir: That's what you think.

… has now become a way of life.

Much of this might be put down to the way work under capitalism has bloated into an inescapable totality, one which is universally loathed yet seemingly without any alternative. A suitable soundtrack to this impasse can be found in the laconic verse of the young Michel Houellebecq. Awaking from a troubled and lonely sleep, contemplating the drab commute to the central business district followed by yet another meaningless day's work, the poet opines:

The morning. Explosions. Blue everywhere. Always blue; magnificent. The new day unrelenting. When will life be gentle? When will I be dead?

This is not simply the morose reverie of an overpaid, suicidal banker. The pathos of Houellebecq's poetry lies in the way it conveys the feeling that there is a fate far worse than death. From the daily tedium of the office, to the humiliating team building exercise, to the alienating rituals of the service economy, to the petty mind games of a passive-aggressive boss: the experience is not one of dying ... but neither of living. It is a *living death*. As Houellebecq recently said in an interview with the *Paris Review*: 'Entering the workforce is like entering the grave ... From then on, nothing happens and you have to pretend to be interested in your work.' Although dead, we are nevertheless compelled to wear the exterior signs of life. Recognizing that workers at heart feel lifeless has prompted a new wave of managerial motivation techniques gleaned from the growing industry of self-help and new-age spirituality. The corporation now hires 'fun-sultants', whose job is to design puerile office games to make us laugh as we work ourselves to death. The now ubiquitous ideology of 'liberation management' has realized that no one can exploit workers better than workers themselves ('leave them alone and they will work forever'). And the trend of injecting authenticity and other life affirming moments into work is a central facet of modern managerialism.

But these tricks only end in humiliation. Every worker knows that the rituals of capitalism are inherently against life, even if repackaged in miniature Buddhas on the computer monitor. In the grave, at least no one expects a pretty smile or a half-baked joke. When the economy of work infects one's early morning dreams, spills over into booze-soaked weekends and reduces almost every social relation to a cold cash exchange, workers are the first to realize that life becomes evacuated, a perpetual living absence no matter how many smiley-faces dot the cubicle. As T.W. Adorno wryly noted in his strikingly prescient analysis of late capitalism, the fact that we continue to live in this petrified air merely indicates that we have learnt to breathe in hell.

What is it about working today that produces a person who exists between life and death, a figure whose only hope is that it might soon all be over? In some ways the dead man working is not an entirely new species. Some enduring features of capitalism are still important to consider here. Karl Marx first revealed the peculiar *self-referentiality* of our society, a remarkable feature which entailed a qualitative shift in social experience. Whereas most other cultures seem to place something beyond itself to garner motivation – the gods, the supernatural, utopia and so-forth – capitalism exists only for itself. It has become its own final destination. As Marx sighed, this makes for a 'sad materialism', because a life determined by the repetitive loop of work and consumption takes us nowhere. Hence the old union lament: 'do we exist simply to work, or do we work so that we can live?'

To compensate for this dead end nature of capital, we have been witnessing the birth of a new culture industry with its artificial zones of 'leisure', whose rationale has been to provide a momentary escape from a society without purpose. Only then can we say: the reason we work is to spend money on something meaningful, be it holidays, our kids or video games. And we might also view the clumsy attempts of industrial psychologists to create spaces of externality as part of this fantasy of a world beyond work. Of course, most employees know this is a swindle. The things in life we could look forward to, beyond the daily grind, are few and often sadly mundane. Consider the scene from the post-apocalyptic film, *Children of Men*; the film's alcoholic anti-hero, Theo, captures the experience perfectly when talking to his friend Jasper:

> Jasper: What did you do for your birthday?
> Theo: Nothing, just like any other day
> Jasper: You must have done something?
> Theo: Nope. Woke up, felt like shit. Went to work, felt like shit.
> Jasper: That's called a hangover, amigo
> Theo: At least with a hangover I feel something.
> Jasper: You should come and live with me.
> Theo: Why would I do that? Then I would have absolutely nothing to look forward to.

How do we cope, when the only thing we could still look forward to is a short retreat to the countryside to visit our pot-smoking middle-aged hippie friend? In the same way as with any other soul-deadening activity, through minor thought games, escapism, sexual fantasies, pranks and jokes. But ultimately, by numbing ourselves and *waiting for it to end*. This is why the greatest fear of today's managers is not absenteeism like it was in the halcyon days of Fordism. In a new culture of work that demands every fiber of your organism to always be switched on, the enemy to production is what human resource managers like to call *presenteeism*: being present only in body with every other part of you being far, far away (on a beach, making love, setting a building on fire, etc.) This is why even a child knows that the smile and 'have a great day' from a customer-service-worker is fundamentally creepy. Not only is it obvious that they don't mean it (and why should they?) but there doesn't seem to be anyone actually behind the smile.

But only with the advent of the postmodern 'social factory', in which every waking (and as we shall see in the next chapter, sleeping) moment becomes a time of work, does the dead man working truly appear. Many commentators today, most notably Michael Hardt and Antonio Negri, have argued that capitalist economic rationality has escaped the factory and offices to become the template for all facets of society. What others have called *24 hour capitalism* not only means that at any moment of the day (and night) someone, somewhere is working but also that at any moment of the day *everyone is always working*.

The real fault-line today is not between capital and labor. It is between *capital and life*. Life itself is now something that is plundered by the corporation, rendering our very social being into something that makes money for business. We know them. The computer hackers dreaming code in their sleep. The airline stewards evoking their warm personality to deal with an irate customer ('act as if the airplane cabin is your living room'). The aspiring NGO intern working for nothing. The university lecturer writing in the weekend. The call center worker improvising on the telephone to enhance the customer experience.

What makes capitalism different today is that its influence reaches far beyond the office. Under Fordism, weekends and leisure time were still relatively untouched. Their aim was to indirectly support the world of work. Today, however, capital seeks to exploit our very sociality in *all* spheres of life. When we all become 'human capital' we not only have a job, or perform a job. We *are* the job. Even when the work-day appears to be over. This is what some have called the rise of bio-power, where life itself is put to work: our sociality, imagination, resourcefulness, and our desire to learn and share ideas. But as we all know, modern corporations cannot provide these drivers of value by their own accord. That's why *we* are enlisted to do it for them. Self-exploitation has become a defining motif of working today. Indeed, the reason why so little is invested by large companies into training is because they have realized that workers *train themselves*, both on the job, using their life skills and social intelligence, and away from the job, on their own time.

So does the dead man working fight back? Is he trying to change his predicament? He is still waiting for the end, but when he realizes that it may not come, resistance becomes a matter of *inducing an end*. The perplexing question running through the pages of this book is the following: how can we resist capitalism when it has penetrated our very mode of social being? Perhaps the old Marxist argument about class politics still holds true. Being a worker is nothing to be proud of. Meaningful workplace politics ought not to be calling for fairer work, better work, more or less work, but *an end to work*. Might this also mean the end of the worker? Finding himself paralyzed, crippled, and only half alive, the dead man working has sought to reinvent death by crafting his own private terminus, a final conclusion to what he is. Worryingly, many of these escape attempts are not pretty, involving mind-numbing drugs, self-loathing, aerobics and suicide (as recently witnessed at France Télécom and elsewhere).

Now we must make a harrowing journey through the petrified world of dead work. And although it has not yet arrived, we can see it coming. The wave is gathering strength and sometimes seems close and other times still far off. Will it ever arrive?

2

'Mainlining' Life into Dead Labor

The screwball characters of the child/adult's television programme *The Muppet Show* might seem far from the stupefying atmosphere of the modern corporation. But capitalism has become strange. While work is still something we would rather avoid like the plague, the tyrannical boss has been replaced by another figure: the passive aggressive Human Resource Manager. Armed with the latest kitchen-sink psychology, and behaving like David Brent from *The Office*, convinced that his real talents lie in performance art, this new architect of corporate culture attempts to convince workers that they should enjoy their own exploitation. Their aim is clear. Not only to make us do something we would rather shun, but also make us *want to do it*.

Picture the scene: On a chilly Monday morning a group of twelve call center workers feel a twinge of anxiety as they leave their 'call-pods' and file into a large meeting room. The firm – let us call it 'Sunray Customer Service' – are well informed about the alienating nature of labor, especially when it comes to the mind numbing, depressing and frequently humiliating job of a call center slave. But Sunray management had a clever idea. Knowing that it was only when its workers had checked-out (either literally or mentally) that they begin to feel human again and buzz with life; knowing, also, that call center work requires high levels of social intelligence, innovation and emotional initiative; knowing all these things, Sunray had to find a way of capturing and replicating that buzz of life … on the job.

Capitalism has always destroyed the thing it needs the most. But when it is the very humanity of the employee – his or her capacity to communicate, think creatively and be social – an array of hired occupational scientists have attempted the impossible: to *inject life into the dead-zone of work*. Managers at Sunray were rabid enthusiasts of this human technology. It encouraged employees to treat the call center as if it was their home or a late night party. As the training manuals and motivation talks relentlessly reminded them:

> Most call centers treat their employees like battery hens. Not Sunray. We are free rangers and respect that everyone is different and special.

The mantra repeated in an Orwell-meets-Oprah manner was 'Just be yourself!' All of those elements of personality that were once barred from work – sexuality, lifestyle, fashion tastes, obsessions with pop stars and health food – have now become welcome, if not demanded, on the job. If you are gay, that's great! If you hate capitalism, wonderful! If you are of Nepalese ethnic descent, perfect! For there is no better call center worker than one who can improvise around the script, breathe life into a dead role and pretend their living death is in fact the apogee of life.

Back to the Sunray meeting-room on that cool Monday morning. The workers looked at the floor anxiously, feigning smiles but knowing that something pretty awful was about to happen. They were told to form a circle as Carla – the 'team development leader' – prepared to deliver a pep-talk, which would have been funny if not for the sadistic glint in her eye. 'As you all know, life at Sunray is more than just a job, it's all about fun and enjoying yourself, here you can really shine and be yourself!' The workers shifted nervously as she bleated on, 'And it's all about color and fun … OK guys, lets do it!'. 'Oh Jesus' muttered one worker with blue hair and an anarchist tattoo on his wrist. Carla hit PLAY on her outdated CD player and we all began to sing Kermit the Frog's only Top-10 single: *Why are there, so many, songs about rainbows, what makes the world go round …*

someday we'll find it, the rainbow connection, the lovers, the dreamers and me ...

This team building exercise, which one of the authors observed when studying new methods of exploitation in the service sector, seems remote from the large-scale power shifts reshaping a waning late-capitalism. However, we suggest that it is indicative of how novel forms of regulation are focusing on those moments of life that once flourished beyond the remit of the corporation. Like a desperate junkie that resorts to 'mainlining' (injecting straight into the vein) to sustain an unsustainable condition, moribund-style capitalism is attempting to revive its flagging fortunes by turning to that which it has always killed ... living labor. We know from Marx's prophetic study of capital that living labor is its central source of value. This is defined primarily by movement and sociality, our creation of a common world – *our* world – that is rich with reciprocal social relations, networks of co-operation and mutual aid. *This is the ironic communist underbelly of capitalism.* On the outside, capital may seem fluid, dynamic and full of creative possibilities, but that is part of its mythology. In fact the opposite is evident once we free our selves from the mentality of work. Marx is clear on this point. What to us appears to be a creative movement – the essence of life itself – is in fact a cunning ruse fabricated by the frenetic and goal orientated nature of *speed-labor*. Despite all the hustle, nothing really changes. Only when the sleeper awakes and soberly considers life from the position of non-work does the figure of the dead man working come into sharp relief. Perhaps what is different today, however, is the crucial ideological function that the fantasy of 'non-work' plays. Ironically, imagining ourselves elsewhere only binds us tighter to that which we seek to escape.

The corporation's turn to those living moments that persist beyond the dead lands of economic rationality indicates a major shift in the nature of power at work today. Sunray's idiotic evocation of *The Muppets* is a far cry from how work used to be organized. The proto-typical factory supervisor or office manager considered play, humour, sexuality and personal idiosyncrasies an impediment to the rational pursuit of productivity. The 'human factor' still existed of course, flourishing beneath the radar in informal games and sub-cultures, but management viewed this as a dangerous underworld of autonomy. Something to be eradicated. Consider the 1960s factory depicted in Huw Beynon's classic *Working for Ford* (where workers were admonished with the motto: 'when we are at work, we work, when that is done only then can we play'). Or consider Max Weber's dark description of the bureaucratic office and its systematic annihilation of love, passion and individuality. All of this is a universe away from working at Sunray. Even the 1980s IBM-led 'corporate culture' craze, which modelled the enterprise after the family, maintained a sharp line between work and non-work. This separation was observed by Gideon Kunda in his famous study, *Engineering Culture*, where he recalls one employee chastising a co-worker who had confessed that overwork had driven him to alcoholism: 'you keep that kind of shit to yourself.' At Sunray, however, anything and everything personal – warts and all – was welcome. Why this sea change in managerial thought and the rules of exploitation?

The reason is two-fold. Firstly, it relates to a crisis of capital that compels it to search for a spark of life at work in increasingly desperate ways. Secondly, the *virus of being at work* has spread throughout the social body, seeking more and more uncommercial moments to make money from. A good starting point to unravel this transformation is the *crisis* of Fordism. From the 1970s and into the 1980s Western capitalism was rocked by a number of crises that were internal (debt and stagnation) and external (the oil embargo). It could no longer organize itself and generate the rate of profit required. Two important developments followed. First, the deindustrialization of the West and the

concomitant growth of service work; second, and more importantly for us, the displacement of the management function onto
labor itself. Indeed, capital realized it could no longer organize
itself; thus, better to enlist the workforce to carry out the job
themselves. This massive dependency on labor could have
hastened the end of work and the sweet abolition of capital
forever. But it didn't.

One only has to turn to academic work to see how this
involves a substantial change in power relations whereby work
becomes a continuous *way of life*, rather than just something we
do among other things. The academic today dutifully writes his
lectures on a Sunday night, explores new ideas while half asleep,
arrives at class punctually, trains himself in the art of writing,
reading, and communicating. As a result the corporatized
university makes grotesque surpluses out of a self-fashioned
craft (and, yes, it is sadly ironic that one of the authors is writing
this sentence on a very sunny Easter Friday). This typifies how
hierarchies of regulation have been *horizontalized*. Most of us still
have a boss above us giving orders. But we have also partially
internalized this 'boss function'. Whereas under Fordism
workers could mentally tell the boss to 'fuck off' as they left the
factory, now they take it home with them. Turning-off is no
longer an available option. Might not this be capitalism's
ultimate Frankensteinian moment? (Recall the curse
Frankenstein received from his jilted monster: *I shall be with you
on your wedding night!*)

This might be one reading of Gilles Deleuze's classic essay
'Postscript on the Societies of Control.' Whereas Foucault argued
that the template of the prison had permeated all of society
including the factory, Deleuze surmised he had got it the wrong
way around. It was the factory – not an actual factory, but the
factory in its *virtual form*, as a way of life, a gaseous ethos – that
has infected our biosphere. When we breathe the molecules of
the social foundry, we always 'owe the man', are indebted to the

boss, the master. The sheer totality of this state of affairs is what makes Deleuze paranoid:

> In a society of control, the corporation has replaced the factory, and the corporation is a spirit, a gas … In the disciplinary societies one was always starting again (from school to the barracks, from the barracks to the factory), while in the societies of control one is never finished with anything – the corporation, the educational system, the armed services being metastable states coexisting in one and the same modulation, like a universal system of deformation.

The traditional line-in-the-sand between capital and labor no longer makes sense to anyone. Today, the real struggle is between capital and *life* (bios), although the struggle is not played out under especially fair rules, given that we can hardly tell what life is anymore. We should consider here what Foucault and his followers have called *bio-power*. If work was once primarily regulated by bureaucracy through depersonalization then today we witness the emergence of a new regime of control which we call *biocracy*, in which life itself is an essential 'human resource' to be exploited.

Perhaps this is why we find our sentimental friend, Kermit the Frog, entering the call center as a vehicle for tapping into the life force of labor. This is not an isolated case. Life itself is now the most lucrative kind of capital being put to work, from the hipster-marketing firm to the call center sweatshop. Work is now presented as the Siamese twin to life, as the sphere in which life can most fully thrive. Personal preferences of the employee of the month – choice of music, favourite food, and historical heroes – are presented on a monitor in the office's foyer. And workers are encouraged to bring personal items to work. Pictures of beloved children and dogs, a banner of the favourite football team and souvenirs bought from that distant holiday in Lanzarote are intermingled with piles of paper in the cubicle. Moreover, pop-management books abound on the topic of play, fun and authenticity with the hope of rendering work into a paradoxical moment of non-work. In his best seller, *The Seven Day Weekend*, management guru Ricardo Semler argues that work and life are now one. The blurb on the back cover is telling:

> Imagine a company where employees set their own hours; where there are no offices, no job titles, no business plans; where employees get to endorse or veto any new venture; where kids are encouraged to run the halls; and where the CEO lets other people make nearly all the decisions ... if you have the freedom to get your job done on your own terms and to blend your work life and personal life with enthusiasm and creative energy. Smart bosses will eventually realize that you might be most productive if you work on Sunday afternoon, play golf on Monday morning, go to a movie on Tuesday afternoon, and watch your child play soccer on Thursday.

It is easy to see why some workers lament the good old days when at least they could leave their kids at home rather than be hounded by them at the office as well! But does this mean that work and life might now be somehow reconciled, that a 'frictionless capitalism' has finally arrived? No. This trend is pure ideology since it seeks to intensify our unfreedom in the language of non-work. Yet work remains in its Deleuzian 'gaseous' form, which is the exact opposite of play, fun, and real living. Therefore, the latter needs to be staged, manufactured, scripted and ultimately *imitated* in the office. As the Sunray call center example indicates, the obvious weakness of this manufactured and faux life resides in its coercive nature. Employees have little choice but to participate in yet another humiliating team-building exercise. If asked to wear their pyjamas to work (on the much dreaded 'pyjama day') or sing a silly Muppets song, they had better not object. Being a party-pooper is today the most serious crime you could commit, even worse than taking these exercises to the extreme (wearing an indecently provocative pyjama, or singing in the exact, unbearably loud and shrill, voice of the Muppets). Herein lies a curious aspect of *biocracy*, what we might call a *formalized informality*. You are forced, weirdly, to be yourself. And what other response could be made to this ridiculous demand than the one already made by our anarchist worker, when he forlornly mumbled 'Oh, Jesus …'? (And no, he was not considering this a serious cry for help; he was a committed atheist)

Extending workplace regulation by imitating life serves an important economic role when capitalism becomes super-reliant on human qualities like social intelligence, reciprocity, communication and shared initiative. These aspects of being human often lie outside or beyond the logic of economic rationality, as Paulo Virno succinctly puts it:

> The productive cooperation in which labor-power participates is always larger and richer than the one put into play by the labor process. It includes also the world of non-labor, the experiences and knowledge matured outside of the factory and the office. Labor-power increases the value of capital only because it never loses its qualities of non-labor.

This places the corporation in a precarious position. After all, it is only that which is non-exploited, non-controlled and freely expressed which can provide the raw material for 'cognitive capitalism' today – a basic requirement of even the most menial work, as our call center example reveals. Indeed, social intelligence often develops *despite* the regulations of the typical workplace, not because of them. Peter Blau observed this in his classic study of office politics in the 1960s. In an attempt to convey their discontent, employees did something strange: *exactly what they were told to do, following the formal rules to the letter.* As a result, when the invisible wealth of informal engagement, knowledge sharing, and mutual aid was withdrawn, the office was brought to a halt. The implications of Blau's study is clear: the formal corporate form actually *obstructs* the creation of wealth, and is thus completely reliant on an undercurrent of non-commercialized living labor, the very thing it cannot help but demolish as soon as it gets its anxious hands on it.

It is now fairly obvious what was happening at the Sunray call center. Here, the demand to 'just be yourself' was nothing but a cunning way of capturing the much needed sociality of the employee: affability on the phone, friendliness, and intuition – all of which are crucial in interactive customer service work. Importantly, this transforms our vision of the corporation from something that *creates* value to something that *encloses* it. As Lazzarato argues, 'the enterprise does not create its object (goods) but *the world within which the object exists* ... the enterprise does not create its subjects (workers and consumers) but *the world within which the subject exists*.' For us, however, Lazzarato seems to be ceding too much credit to the corporation. As Marx's thesis on dead labor implies, capital can't even create these two worlds, since only living entities can make a world, a home, a space and time of co-existence.

Finally, this displacement of non-work into the office also entails the obverse, the shift of work into all pockets of life. As we have already demonstrated, our so-called 'worker's society' is a hermeneutically sealed totality in which *we are always at work.* And therefore always entangled in a moment of living death. The traditional point of production – say the factory assembly line – is scattered to every corner of our lives since it is our very sociality that creates value for business. As Andrew Ross noted in his study of the IT firm Razorfish, 'ideas and creativity were just as likely to surface at home or in other locations, and so employees were encouraged to work elsewhere ... the goal was to extract value from every waking moment of an employee's day.'

But it is not only when this new bio-political proletariat is awake that they are working. Value is being created even in their most intimate and vulnerable states, when asleep. This is vividly captured in a recent biographical essay by Rob Lucas, 'Dreaming in Code'. The computer programmer described how his life was so integrated with his job that sleep was even involved, dreaming up solutions to complex code conundrums (what he called 'sleep working') in the middle of the night. He writes, 'dreaming about your work is one thing, but dreaming inside the logic of your work is another ... in the kind of dream I have been having the very movement of my mind is transformed: it has become that of my job.' Such 'sleep working' was not experienced as an amplification of life. On the contrary, it represented a subtraction, a vampire-like negation of his vital existence for the benefit of an impersonal and repellent institutional imposition. A job.

* * *

As exploitation is generalized in time and space like an invisible gas, an absolute worker's society emerges, a society in which neither life nor death appears on the horizon. We know this place. We know the smell and taste of the perpetual living death in the office, on the commuter bus, in the dark mine, or the restroom of an empty office tower in the middle of the night - even in our dreams.

3

Under the Paving-Stones, the Corporation!

The December 2010 protests in London, prompted by university spending cuts, saw the streets around the Parliament buildings become a major site of conflict, involving thousands of demonstrators and an intimidating police presence. As night fell, things got nasty. One of the authors meandered through the crowd, and as violence seemed imminent, rather cowardly sought shelter in the doorway of a nearby pub. A formation of riot police arrived – dressed in black with faces covered in menacing masks – and positioned themselves a stone's throw away from the make-shift sanctuary. They were surveying a seething and indistinguishable crowd of demonstrators moving in the darkness of Trafalgar Square. And then, almost inaudibly, one could hear a collective whisper: 'Little pig, little pig ... let me in!' This dangerous situation merged with memories of childhood trepidation for an instant as the police disappeared into the black night with batons poised.

An unnerving encounter for sure in which state violence was raw and uncompromising in its display. While the police and demonstrators were clashing, an underground magazine expressing leftwing, anti-corporate views – particularly popular in the bohemian corners of East London – saw a unique opportunity. It was not to snap an image of excessive police brutality or interview protestors for an article on the degradation of university education. No, what they saw was the perfect backdrop for a photo-shoot, with beautiful young models advertising the latest chic underground labels. Standing in front of an angry mob we see Aza. She wears a wonderful coat from *Beyond Retro*, a vintage t-shirt from *Rokit*, a vintage skirt from *Mint*, a

Rellik vintage scarf and *Pretty Polly* tights. Standing beside a heavily armored riot cop (who has a look of mild confusion on his face) is Ertie. She wears a *Lavenham* coat, a jacket from *McQ*, a *Joseph* dress, *Pretty Polly* tights and *Dr. Martens* shoes. And posing precariously near a burning public bench that is also being kicked by a demonstrator for good measure is Scarlett. She wears a *Peter Jensen* dress, a *Top Shop* coat, tights from *Pretty Polly* (obviously a favorite among the leftwing hipster set), *American Apparel* socks, and shoes from *Vans*. Revolution, it seems, is now the stage for a new kind of catwalk.

These images of countercultural resistance, ironically mixed up in a commercial and pro-business language, might appear as a satirical image of postmodern commodification. But there is something else going on here, too. It signals the emergence of a new brand of capitalist ideology, especially as it pertains to sprouting modes of work and the persona we have set out to understand: the dead man working. For many years, capitalism fought an ideological battle around its legitimation that was staunchly rightwing in nature. Criticism was the reserve for those on the left who were worried about the alienating and disenfranchising effects of large enterprise, market society and class inequalities. Corporate ideology, on the other hand, aimed to justify the sanctity of markets by painting the business world in glowing colors (as the creator of jobs, wealth, social goods). However, since the 1990s a strange mutation has occurred. What Tom Wolfe dubbed 'radical chic' in his classic 1970s *New Yorker* article (lambasting the trend of privileged elites holding tea-parties with radical militants to revive their waning artistic kudos) has now been mainstreamed in the imagery of corporate life. When it comes to mainlining life into the dead man working, it is not only *non-work* that has been harnessed to deepen the edifice of employment, but crucially, *anti-work*. It seems that subversion – in a harmless and defanged form – is a real seller.

Even a cursory glance at popular culture today shows how

society has set upon the corporation and its meaningless jobs. Criticism has become commonplace, and is now available to see in Hollywood blockbusters like *Office Space, Erin Brockovich, The Constant Gardener, The Insider,* as well as documentaries such as *Capitalism: A Love Story, The Corporation* and *Super Size Me.* But this is cinema. How about the real world of work? Thomas Frank spotted the unlikely symbiosis between anti-work and the ethos of industrious labor in the 1990s. In *The Conquest of Cool* he shows how some key leftist motifs like emancipation, free self-expression and anti-authoritarianism had been co-opted by modern management discourse. Rather than radicalism being silenced as a dangerous or subversive element, it is now welcomed in cardboard cut-out form, even featuring in the boardroom. Take Frank's observation about how anti-establishment sentiment and nouvelle managerialism joined forces to invent 'liberation management':

Beginning in 1991-92 (when *Nevermind* ascended the Billboard charts and Tom Peters' *Liberation Management* appeared), American popular culture and corporate culture veered off together on a spree of radical sounding bluster that mirrored the events of the 1960s so closely as to make them seem almost unremarkable in retrospect. Caught up in what appeared to be an unprecedented prosperity driven by the 'revolutionary' forces of globalization and cyber-culture, the nation became obsessed with youth culture and the march of generations ... In business literature, dreams of chaos and ceaseless undulation routed the 1980s dreams of order and 'excellence'.

Perhaps elegiac Kurt Cobain-types are now ideal pinup models for an unconventional kind of management consultant, one who hates the firm while simultaneously being supine and conformist. The ultra-conservative analyst David Brooks, in his glorification of 'Bobos' (or the bohemian bourgeois) even says this ethos of counter-management, replete with anarchist ideals, is the leading ideological form of the corporation today:

> If you want to find a place where the Age of Aquarius radicalism is in full force, you have to go higher up the corporate ladder into the realm of companies listed on the New York Stock Exchange. Thirty years after Woodstock and all the peace rallies, the people who talk most relentlessly about smashing the status quo and crushing the establishment are management gurus and corporate executives.

This peculiar kind of anti-corporate business ideology is now found everywhere. When passing through the airports of Europe, North America and elsewhere, one of the more unsavory elements of the authors' work is to reluctantly visit the 'business section' of departure lounge bookshops. While most other travellers browse through more cultivated tomes, we instead purchase off-putting titles like *Management by Fun* or *The Four Minute Work Week* and other cheap paperbacks that proclaim the final arrival of a Gatesean era of frictionless capitalism. Leading this throng of pop-management pundits is Tom Peters and his hugely influential notion of 'liberation management'. Peters' argument is that management should not be about visibly controlling people, telling them what to do or smothering them with useless bureaucracy and lines of authority. Instead, the new 'firm with a soul' ought to unleash what people already are, with all of their authentic, diverse and idiosyncratic features on display. Only then, when the worker is 'free', can creativity, innovation and free-thinking thrive.

A major aspect of liberation management is to harness the edgy and non-conformist energy of workers. Large firms, the advice says, ought to model their internal structures after the carnivalesque and joyous anarchism of May '68. They should hire anti-authoritarians and even indolent employees who hate everything about capitalism, including the very corporation that has hired them. These types of workers will create the most value because they are not simply telling management what it wants to hear, faking conformity and getting through yet another pointless day by doing the bare minimum. They also contribute things the corporation could not provide on its own accord: life. The fact that they are cynical and overtly against their own employer poses no problem. Because they're not going anywhere.

Of course, what the ideology of liberation management does not tell us is that all the old excessive structures of control remain intact. Workers are bossed around by old fashion bureaucrats and Hitler-like micromanagers more now than ever. But they are done so whilst perversely being ordered to speak their mind, exude authenticity and have fun. The catchphrase of May '68 radicalism cried that under the paving-stones of the cold corporate metropolis were the warm beaches of freedom. Today, however, what we will find under the paving-stones is yet another level of the multinational firm itself, this time draped in the guise of an EasyJet holiday destination.

How are we to make sense of this development at a theoretical level? Radical philosophy has always been worried about the way in which its own mental co-ordinates might be acceded by the commodity form. This is especially so given the supple and expansive nature of capitalism: it is able to commodify anything, even, ironically, anti-capitalism itself, as millions of Che Guevara T-shirts attest. Adorno perhaps explored this problem in greater detail than anyone else. For him, the esoteric task of what he coined 'negative dialectics' was to discover a distant signal of otherness in the act of negation. But as Adorno pushed dialectics to its ultimate limit, it eventually imploded under the pressure. We then enter a world of pure, unadulterated power. As he sadly puts it, the detached observer is as much entangled as the active participant; the only advantage of the former is insight into his entanglement, and the infinitesimal freedom that lies in knowledge as such. His own distance from business at large is a luxury which only that business confers.

While these heady-heights of philosophical reflection left many in a state of torpor, a new culture of criticism emerged in the 1960s among the youth and civil rights movements that defied traditional class politics. The student movement in particular rejected the very nature of daily life under corporate rule. It was boring, dull and exceedingly depressing. The old stereotype of the 'organization man' who was content to deny himself 'a life' suddenly became the enemy, scorned as an obsolete square, hopelessly out of sync with the generational refusal of work.

As the police yet again appeared in the streets of London, Paris, New York and Berlin to remind everyone who was boss, vast amounts of ideological activity was afoot at the heart of the corporation. In their archival study of management thought, Boltanski and Chiapello argue that the 'new spirit of capitalism' was being designed to pre-empt what then appeared as a dangerous criticism. The result was a novel kind of management-speak that openly expressed concerns about the alienating and stupefying effects of work. Now line-managers and tyrannical team leaders began parroting phrases that might only have been found in critical theory manifestos or Situationist fliers calling for a mass *détournement*. As Boltanski and Chiapello observe, 'to maintain its power of attraction, capitalism therefore has to draw upon resources external to it, beliefs which, at a given moment in time, possess considerable powers of persuasion ... even when they are hostile to it.' This truly resulted in what we might call a 'Marx for managers'.

The ideological coup is two-fold. First is the appearance of a seemingly humanized mode of work ('friendly capitalism').

Second is the shift of attention to the subjective ills of work, which detracts from the real enemy: the objective, concrete preponderance of corporate exploitation and regulation. Like liberalism itself, this ideology was able to conjure an image of care while continuing to rely on pure force and coercion. Perhaps one of the best depictions of this 'new spirit of capitalism' can be found in Andrew Ross' fascinating insider's account of Razorfish. This firm completely blurred the work/non-work boundaries, akin to the call center we discussed earlier. 'Neo-leisure' especially saturated the climate inside the enterprise, sitting alongside a regime of long, arduous labor. What made Razorfish particularly interesting was the value placed on 'transgression' and 'permissiveness' by management: the offices were located in warehouses near the artistic area of town, left only partially renovated to inspire a feeling of artisanal amateurness and chic underground cool, and the firm openly supported socially progressive and even anti-corporate causes. Ross memorably labels this the 'industrialization of bohemia', as it traded heavily on an aesthetic of radicalism.

Managers aimed to create a climate that conveyed a communal and playful tone that was once anathema to traditional corporate life. Some employees even portrayed themselves as performers of a subversive type of living. When he describes the kind of employees at Razorfish, the signs of counterculture are redolent: 'rule breaking, undisciplined, self-dramatizing, sexually free, drug using, youthfully merry, inadvisably honest, unorthodox in their narcissism, and neo-socialist in their sense of community.' But above all, this fashionable display of dissent keys directly into maintaining a routine of hard labor. To paraphrase Ross: 'giving the finger to corporate America was a big boost for recruitment and employee morale.'

The reference to 'neo-socialism' here resonates with what Žižek sees as the coming era of the 'liberal communist.' This figure signifies the ultimate neoliberal moment, in which pro-market industrialists and entrepreneurs deploy the phraseology of ethical business, poverty alleviation and egalitarianism. Whereas capitalism used to justify itself by denying the existence of its foundational moment of violence, today it has changed tack to openly address the harm of business, but with some surprising and counterintuitive results – that is, deepening its power over the world and imagination without the slightest modification in its basic operating principles.

Bob Geldof and Bono might be seen as chief personifications of the liberal communist, using their philanthropy to frame the carnage of global capitalism as but exceptional aberrations from an otherwise sound state of affairs. Of course, this detracts from the truth: all of these so-called rare exceptions are in fact axiomatic to markets and the transnational corporation, without which they could not exist. The liberal communist, however, wishes us to believe that we can enjoy the selfish rewards of rampant profiteering and eat our cake too, basking in the euphoric afterglow that comes when one 'cares for society'. We might call this blinding fantasy the 'Bonofication' of capitalist reality.

The ideology of liberal communism is no better exemplified than by the widespread prevalence of Corporate Social Responsibility. We would be hard pressed to find any firm today that did not have some blurb on its website or induction manual about how it is 'giving back' to society and aspiring to be sustainable. But as numerous studies have demonstrated, the multinationals that have the most lush and grandiose Corporate Social Responsibility policies are precisely those which do the most damage: petroleum companies, tobacco firms and so-forth. While we might see British Petroleum's recent attempt to rebrand itself as Beyond Petroleum (complete with a green flower) as a cynical PR exercise, it is the function that this 'ideology of care' has *inside the firm* that is crucial. The language of ethics, sharing and social responsibility appears strangely attractive to the disaffected post-industrial employee. Managers have a problem: how do we connect with a generation of workers who think capitalism is not only a dead end, but fundamentally destructive to society and nature? This is when appeals to Corporate Social Responsibility and its *discourse of the social* become vital in the postmodern enterprise.

Jana Costas' study of a notoriously pugnacious management consultancy firm in London found that Corporate Social Responsibility was crucial for realigning the disengaged employee with an awful business model. She observed a raft of social responsibility initiatives such as the use of Fair Trade in the cafeteria, sabbaticals for employees to work in Africa, and community-care-days – all of which aimed to reconcile the worker with a job which is fundamentally at odds with his values and ideals. The work was dull, yes, but the culture was also extremely anti-social, particularly disaffecting the signif-icant number of staff recruited from the humanities (with degrees, for example, in politics, English and philosophy). The pseudo counter-capitalist values conveyed in the Corporate Social Responsibility discourse provided one way to square the socially progressive expectations of an educated workforce (some of whom even reported that at heart they were 'commu-nists').

Costas gives us a poignant example. Paul is a mild-mannered and rather sensitive employee who found his job completely onerous and devoid of anything remotely connected to being human. He had a degree in philosophy from a very prestigious university, subscribed to the *London Review of Books* (which largely remained unopened given the hours he spent at work) and held relatively leftwing views about business and society. This is how he described his life in the organization:

I find the overall work here quite limiting and quite constricting, but if you push it I would say that I find the work quite asphyxiating. That basically means 'strangling'. The sort of feeling that it constricts you. I often find myself to be getting stupider. Those things, like reading and learning new languages, are still very important to me and I just can't, I just don't have that room in my personal life to keep it up while working for the firm. I describe it as being brain-rotten.

The imagery here is dramatic, with strong feelings of self-alienation. It was exactly this kind of employee that the Corporate Social Responsibility policy was geared for. Paul found solace and reconciliation in the 'business ethics' of the corporation as it provided the illusion that he was not a hypocrite after all. He said that the sabbatical and away days in which they collected rubbish in the streets of East London made his suffering worthwhile.

Perhaps this is why Žižek calls environmentalism *the new opium of the masses*, in which the apparent openness about the social harms of corporate power actually functions to obscure its own causes. The hegemony emerging out of the present economic/social crisis is that of a 'socially responsible eco-capitalism' in which collaboration with employees, dialogue with customers, respect for the environment, and transparency are held as key success factors. Žižek writes:

The new ethos of global responsibility is thus able to put capitalism to work as the most efficient instrument of the common good. The basic ideological dispositive of capitalism – we can call it 'instrumental reason', 'technological exploitation', 'individualist greed' or whatever we like – is separated from its concrete socio-economic conditions (capitalist relations of production) and conceived of as an autonomous life or 'existential' attitude which should (and can) be overcome by a new more 'spiritual' outlook, leaving *those very capitalist relations intact*.

Similarly, the business discourse of ecology evokes a pseudo-criticality that numbs us even further, blinding us to the impending disaster of an unsustainable system (with mindless mantras such as 'recycling will save us'). In other words, the disingenuous code of responsibility provides a practical medium for people to express their concerns, but in a manner that precisely consolidates their role as an obedient, productive worker. The sequence is clear. We are enlightened about the catastrophe around us, we embark on a employee-led social responsibility campaign such as jogging to raise money for a local homeless shelter. We are making a difference, but in reality nothing changes for the better. It is this feeling of 'we tried' that allows us to sustain what we know far too well is an unsustainable state of affairs.

It is hard to say whether Adorno scribbled his 'dark theory' with a smile or a downcast frown. But in his most austere moments he seems convinced that even criticism today is gravely sick. It has become a fetish that serves what it seeks to overcome, reproducing the 'dead zone' of work in the garb of revolution. It thus must carefully be rethought if we are not to blindly walk into oblivion while believing we are 'doing the right thing'. For as Heath and Potter rightly observe in their book *The Rebel Sell*, 'consumer capitalism has emerged from countercultural rebellion stronger than it was before.' In other words, the idiom of capital now understands its own criticism better than ever. And this kind of 'false critique' plays a powerful ideological role for deepening our attachment to the dead world of work. This is a time in which grim and downtrodden employees at the heart of corporate hegemony proclaim to be communist. And even the CEO agrees work sucks. Capitalism persists, not despite, but *because* of this mode of critical awareness. Hence, what are we to do?

4

The Inconvenience of Being Yourself

In *Deconstructing Harry*, arguably Woody Allen's last great movie, Harry (a depressed and spiritually bankrupted writer played by Allen himself) asks the prostitute he has just slept with whether she likes her job or not. 'It's ok', she replies, 'it sure beats waitressing.' Harry wryly observes: 'Why does every hooker I sleep with say it beats waitressing? ... waitressing must be the worst goddamn job in the world!' According to the website *worst-jobs.com*, prostitution is in fact the ninth worst job in the world, probably because its only redeeming feature is that that you might have the same fortune as Julia Roberts in *Pretty Woman*. While prostitution is certainly accepted in many corners of the world it has never quite managed to achieve universal appeal. Job security is low, pensions are rare, career options limited, and the actual work content ... not for everyone. All in all, prostitution is not the kind of occupation children usually grow up dreaming of.

Let's turn to a job seemingly far removed from the world of prostitution, that of management consultancy. It's fascinating to note that when asked about their work, consultants often compare themselves to prostitutes. An analyst at one of London's more prestigious firms told the authors about a satirical email circulating among his colleagues depicting them as hookers. According to the text, they, like prostitutes, work odd hours, have no job satisfaction, are super-exploited and are embarrassed to tell people what they do for a living. The email, however, was not circulated by a disgruntled worker hoping to mobilize anger against management. No, its main distributor was a senior partner, who, like his colleagues, openly expressed his feelings about working: it's shit!

At stake here is the shared and universal discontent with work today. Not only are most jobs pointless but they also engender pointless lives. Like prostitutes, consultants see themselves being gradually 'erased' by their work: 'when you leave to go to see a client, you look great, but return looking like hell (compare appearance on Monday a.m. to Friday p.m.)' And they are not the only ones. A week's work – whether in a call center, supermarket or office – takes its toll, both physically and emotionally, with the standard objection being: 'I feel drained, empty … dead'. What is left is something quite alien to the beautiful person we once knew, now worthy of nothing but our condemnation. In classic Freudian terms, we have become that hated other, objectified and externalized. Or, in the more direct words of the feminist Valerie Solanas, 'a worthless piece of shit'. Endeavouring to understand this existential by-product of the workaday, Romanian philosopher E.M. Cioran wrote in *On the Heights of Despair*:

> Work displaces man's center of interest from the subjective to the objective realm of things. In consequence, man no longer takes an interest in his own destiny but focuses on facts and things. What should be an activity of permanent transfiguration becomes a means of exteriorization, of abandoning one's inner self. In the modern world, work signifies a purely external activity; man no longer makes himself through it, he makes things. That each of us must have a career, must enter upon a certain form of life which probably does not suit us, illustrates work's tendency to dull the spirit.

For sure, modern work has always been dangerous. Friedrich Engels' graphic description of the late 19th century working-class in Victorian England does not make for pleasant reading. Harm is everywhere. People die; and they die an awful death at that, somewhat similar to the demise described on the back of today's cigarette packets, slowly and painfully. However, the danger of modern work – or more particularly the kind of office work found in the Western world, and documented in films and television series like *Office Space* and *The Office* – is more explicitly concerned with a dying spirit, a death which can be equally slow and painful.

Perhaps one of the first systematic explorations of how working kills who we are can be found in the American sociologist C. Wright Mills' 1950s classic, *White Collar*. Documenting the fate of saleswomen and salesmen he noted the spread of cynicism and self-loathing. These workers hated their customers, their managers, their jobs, and above all *themselves*. But they made no illusions. They were 'quite aware of the difference between what they really think of the customer and how they must act toward her. The smile behind the counter is a commercialized lure'. As one of the salesgirls explained:

It's really marvellous what you can do in this world with a streamlined torso and a brilliant smile. People do things for me, especially men when I give them that slow smile and look up through my lashes. I found that out long ago, so why should I bother about a variety of selling techniques when one technique will do the trick? I spend most of my salary on dresses which accentuate all my good points. After all, a girl should capitalize on what she has, shouldn't she?

Perhaps modelled on Mills' book, the HBO series *Mad Men*, set in 1960s Madison Avenue, describes the objectification at play in office work. The young provincial girl Peggy, newly appointed as a secretary at the prestigious advertising agency Sterling Cooper, is given a somewhat unconventional introduction. Rather than being introduced to her actual duties, she is taken for an informal tour by a superior secretary. Here, Peggy learns what to wear (skirts showing the knees), how to look at men (ignore them first, then throw them a glance), and how to respond to invitations (don't say yes to all of them, especially not too easily). As a first step in her preparation, Peggy sees the doctor to obtain contraceptive pills – and they come in handy sooner than she would first have thought. She quickly learns the art of exteriorization, to turn herself into an external object – one that can be fucked.

The rub with making the world into objects is that one ends up making oneself an object. A full circle is made. We have become alienated not just from what we produce, as Marx reminded us; nor are we alienated only from our social reality, which has been rendered cold and inhuman. More fundamentally, we are alienated from ourselves.

This is the line of argument found in a wide span of critical thought, from Heidegger and Cioran, through to the Frankfurt School, all the way up to recent sociological works by Richard Sennett and Zygmunt Bauman. The inconvenience found here is one that is concerned with disenchantment and alienation. It is the inconvenience of being inauthentic, *the inconvenience of being what you are not.*

Today, however, our disaffection is much worse. Some thirty years after Mills' exploration of venality among salesmen and women, Arlie Russell Hoschchild, in her book *The Managed Heart,* notes a subtle but significant shift in how we are exploited. What she calls 'emotional labor' is not just about playing well-delineated roles, which can easily be separated from our true sense of self. Through numerous interviews with Delta Airline flight attendants she found that simple acting was not enough. It was insufficient to merely display a fake cheerfulness, as described by Mills. Instead they were requested to wear a more sincere countenance, one that comes through as real and authentic. This transition from acting out scripted roles, to improvised authentic ones, has an obvious rationale. As feelings become a source of value, and thus a commodity to be carefully managed, the greater the need for them to also be authentic, natural, and real. In other words, as Hoschchild states, 'the more the heart is managed, the more we value the unmanaged heart'.

This is what is truly eerie. Following the injunction to be authentic – 'who we truly are' – we can no longer draw the line between what is fake and genuine about ourselves. It isn't just a fake and exteriorized mask that we sell as labor power, but the entire repertoire of our unscreened character, similar to the call center workers discussed earlier who were told to be themselves (or else!). This is where we can begin to discern *the inconvenience of being yourself*.

A deeply troubling inconvenience, no doubt, much more serious than the old problem of self-alienation, of having to be someone we're not. To make this point we need to return to prostitution and a man named Humping Hank, the compassionate and loving whoremonger, the connoisseur kerb-crawler, whose physical appearance is unnervingly similar to Bill Gates.

We meet Hank in one of Louis Theroux's documentaries of American subcultures, as the filmmaker travels to Nevada to visit the Wild Horse Adult Resort & Spa. At the brothel, Louis is introduced to some advanced emotional labor. Under the supervision of the proud Madame, Susan, the girls step forward. One by one, they walk up to Louis, smile invitingly, present themselves – 'Hello, I'm Summer'; Hello, I'm Onyx' – they throw a long and suggestive look, before turning around. 'Isn't that fantastic?', the Madame exclaims, as if she had previously worked for Delta Airlines, training flight attendants, 'they took the time to stop, said their name, gave a beautiful elegant smile: "hey I'm fun"'. 'It allows the girls to show their true personality', Susan continues, explaining how important the introduction is: 'Be fun! Be real! Don't stand there like a plastic Barbie doll!'

Like most brothels, the Wild Horse offers a rich menu of sexual activities, from 'straight lay' (conventional missionary style) to 'crème de menthe French' (oral sex with a sweet liquor chaser). But there is also something else, more exclusive, which can only be offered on request. Like the secret speciality of a chic restaurant, you will not find this service on the menu; it has to be ordered in advance. This speciality is for the initiated known as the GFE: the girlfriend experience. And we soon learn that this is the only service Humping Hank is interested in. He does not fuck the prostitutes like the unrefined truck drivers who call in for a big steak, three beers, and a straight lay. Instead, Hank spends long nights with his 'girlfriend', watching TV, eating popcorn, kissing and hugging, talking about their future, laughing, before time runs out, and he is kissing his beloved goodnight, often with tears in his eyes.

Of course, these emotional laborers dread a visit from Humping Hank since GFE is a violation of their very core, with no protection through role-play. Making matters worse, he is likable, kind and even caring. So no protection through disgust. What we find unique about Humping Hank is the way he captures the spirit of the modern firm with almost perfect precision. He doesn't fuck us and leave us with an unsatisfactory salary, like the capitalism of yesteryear. Instead, he hugs and nurtures us. He tells us how important we are, cares about us, and asks us to be natural and genuine. He encourages us to say anything, because he desires nothing but the unique individual we are. He teaches us, first hand, and in an unambiguous and palpable manner, the inconvenience of being ourselves. Henceforth, our authenticity is no longer a retreat from the mandatory fakeness of the office, but the very medium through which work squeezes the life out of us.

Like Hank, modern employers are not interested in role-play, but demand the real person, the person who jokes, emotes and can think on their feet. The robot-like secretary, with a pasted invariable smile, or one of the all-too-perfect Stepford Wives, with blank empty eyes, is hopelessly outdated in today's workplace. Even Susan, the Madame at the Wild Horse, knows this: don't stand there like a plastic Barbie doll! Be fun! Be real!

What makes the living death of contemporary capitalism especially perverse is the way it kills us with the help of our own longing to be genuine. This goes hand in hand with the way exploitation is organized now. Capitalism has effectively married the emotional skill of being together with the dead calculus of the economy, thus heralding a new type of ideology, close to what Eva Illouz calls 'emotional capitalism'. In the workplace and beyond, people are bombarded from all sides with the injunction to be emotionally promiscuous. The motto is clear: we need to carefully cultivate the unruly and natural sides of our selves to get ahead, and we should never hesitate to bring these to work.

The sociologist Richard Sennett has rightly observed that today it is not your particular skills that will grant success, but your so-called life-skills. To have life-skills equates with being socially malleable, able to display an impervious affection to a task – whatever its nature might be – and then retain that veneer of interest as one swiftly jumps from one job to another. But emotional capitalism does not just prescribe a more open display of warmth and human feeling. It involves what we would like to call *emotional administration*. Human feeling and bureaucratic rationality were once open enemies. But now emotional lives are tightly managed in accordance with a cost-benefit analysis. This is perfectly illustrated by Renata Salecl, in her book *Choice*, where she describes how relationship councillors now advise their clients to manage their romances as a love bank. The idea is simple. When you first meet someone worthy of your interest – a potential partner – you first open up a love account, and start making deposits. You laugh at their jokes (although they are not funny), you buy coffee for them (although you think they could as well buy it themselves), and you massage their feet (although they stink). And in return you can expect the same treatment. In the event of some unforeseen incident – say, for mistaking her wardrobe for a toilet after a long night of binge drinking – the bank account is still sufficiently rich, which gives you some leeway. As soon as you have recovered from the hangover, and the situation has stabilized, you can begin making deposits again – just like a bank account.

Isn't this emotional administration a central characteristic of life in the modern corporation too? As employees, we can no longer happily blend into the anonymous throng of dark suits or blissfully disappear into an indistinguishable mass of factory workers. With the rise of what could only be called *exposure capitalism*, everything about us is suddenly on display – to be seen, to be judged. And with such existential exposure comes a dreadful anxiety – as we saw with the aforementioned call center workers who were forced to sing the 'Rainbow Connection'. Under these conditions there is an ever pressing need to manage *who we are* – our personalities, countenance and self-presentations. But how do we learn this skill? For we all know that being yourself is no easy matter. It is excruciatingly difficult to display unfeigned gratitude to curry the favour of a boss. It is tough to convey genuine humility when persuading a fellow worker to cover for us. And let's not even imagine what it takes to make a creepy client like Humping Hank feel at home. According to Illouz, this world of 'cold intimacies' is inextricably connected with the widespread popularity of therapy (in all its forms, from counselling and yoga to self-help DVDs and life coaching). If therapy promises to discover a route into our authentic self, it also shows us how to manage what we find when we get there.

No one really knows when the corporation suddenly contracted the therapy bug. Some trace it back to a small Californian start-up whose CEO smoked too much pot in the early 1980s. Others point to the personnel manager of a San Francisco coffee chain who got some funny ideas after returning from a holiday with the wife and kids in India. More daring commentators suggest that Patient Zero might have been an ex-football coach who was employed by a large air conditioning retailer on the outskirts of Los Angeles in 1979. But there are two things we do know. First, business coaching and therapy are now a global phenomenon. And second, they have replaced the archetypical 'manager' as the most hated figure in the business firm. From now on, there is no such thing as a bad world, only a bad you. At least in the good old days of Fordism everybody – including managers and owners – knew that work was shit and every sensible person ought to flee from it. No one would have the audacity to persuade you to like it or feel 'at one' with yourself while there. Now things are different. If you are not doing so well, feeling a little down or stressed, having trouble enduring the boss, then a business coach or team councillor is there to tell us: It's not the workplace that's the problem. *It's you.*

Exposing one's authenticity in the workplace might be useful for selling more hair products or climbing the greasy pole, but it must also be seen as a particular expression of power. To understand why, we do well to consult the first volume of the *History of Sexuality*, where Foucault levels an attack on the West's therapeutic culture for this very reason. He notes how the injunction to speak about ourselves, especially in the confessional format, might feel liberating (getting things off our chest, for example). Indeed, everything is allowed; anything can, and ought to, be revealed. There are simply no fantasies too perverse, and no acts too transgressive – all dirty laundry should be aired. The catch, however, is that the confession forces the subject into a power game with terrible odds, as between the suspect and the police in the interrogation room, before the lawyer storms in to silence the all-too-talkative client:

> The confession is a ritual discourse in which the speaking subject is also the subject of the statement; it is also a ritual that unfolds within a power relationship, for one does not confess without the presence (or virtual presence) of a partner who is not simply the interlocutor but the authority which

requires the confession, prescribes and appreciates it, and intervenes in order to judge, punish, forgive, console, and reconcile.

What Foucault was unable to foresee, however, was the reappearance of this authority figure in the garb of a freewheeling liberal (perhaps wearing an ecological caftan). It is not a stern authoritarian that now listens with an expression of deep moralising worry, but a sincerely understanding and permissive manager. The punitive boss who orders us about no longer has much purchase in the postmodern workplace. Rather, we find the manager taking great pains to ask us 'how *we* feel', and 'how *we* would like to interpret the situation'. We might even be encouraged to 'go crazy', which isn't surprising given how our idiosyncrasies and transgressive naughtiness are desired by 'liberation management'. As Žižek remarks, 'I become useless for them [the corporation] the moment I start losing this "imp of perversity", the moment I lose my "countercultural" subversive edge and start to behave like a "normal" mature subject'. One is tempted here to suggest that Freud's superego, traditionally known for its sadistic ways – something like a revengeful priest with a stick – is dead and buried, replaced by a peace-loving hippie on pot, for whom everything goes.

But this redrafting of the superego – like the postmodern manager who also thinks work sucks and rejoices in moments of authenticity – harbours its own brand of sadism. Jacques Lacan demonstrates this by revealing how permissiveness has an obscene underside. Commenting on Dostoevsky's famous line that 'if God doesn't exist … then everything is permitted', Lacan retorts: 'Quite evidently, a naïve notion, for we analysts know full well that if God doesn't exist, then nothing at all is permitted any longer.' Contrary to its overt message, the hippie superego (represented here by our pot-smoking, work-hating postmodern manager) isn't marking the end of prohibition. We still have to follow its command. But now we have to enjoy it too. The command to enjoy, of course, has nothing to do with enjoyment. Sadism comes into the picture precisely because the superego knows very well that this injunction is a cruel joke. As any child who has been ordered by grown ups to enjoy a game knows: the very positioning of the activity within a command structure ruins everything. The gift of freedom, Lacan concluded, swiftly becomes a gift of shit.

Back one last time to Humping Hank and the Wild Horse Adult Resort & Spa. Night has now fallen over the Nevada desert, and Hank and his prostitute girlfriend, Veronica, talk about their long evening together. 'Did I make you forget where you were?', Hank asks smilingly, as he affectionately squeezes her hand. Veronica smiles and nods nervously. She's speechless. She tries her best to explain that the whole thing is professional, a business transaction. But as Hank throws a sad eye, she loses the thread and gives up. If anyone knows the terror of the hippie superego, the inconvenience of being herself, it is Veronica.

Far from the Nevada desert, in the trendiest parts of East London we find another example of the unexpected terror inside the authentic workplace. In the course of a brief stroll through Broadway Market on a Saturday afternoon we run into an array of hipsters, wearing skinny jeans and ironic T-shirts, cruising on their fixed gear bikes. The hipster is famous for embracing everything, while refraining from seriously engaging with anything. As a fuming *Time Out New York* article (prosaically entitled 'Why the hipster must die') puts it: 'under the guise of "irony", hipsterism fetishizes the authentic and regurgitates it with a winking inauthenticity'. It is no wonder that the hipster is now the model employee. While they seem perfectly aware that the frenetic search for authenticity is a dead end, they continue to pursue it nevertheless. Their hyper-reflexivity together with a 'healthy' dose of self-loathing (they embrace YouTube classics like 'Being a Dickhead's Cool' and blogs like *Hackney Hipster*

Hate) makes them the perfect correlates of the hippie superego. They know that their (well paid and uncreative) office job – no, the mainstream hipster is no longer a musician or artist – is not easily compatible with their late-at-night persona. Still, they evidently participate in the fantasy that alienating work can form a frictionless unity with the liberated self. And finally, they know that enjoyment will not be unleashed; yet they happily follow the superego's sadistic injunction: *Enjoy!* Like Veronica, the hipster fully understands the inconvenience of being yourself. But instead of trying to escape that structure (which we assume is Veronica's intention), the hipster voluntarily remains a dead man working.

* * *

Martin Heidegger could not easily have predicted the transformation of work over the course of the last 50 years, although his later texts were written with a pessimistic view of the future. But let us imagine he were miraculously transported into the 21st century and forced to spend a couple of months in a postmodern corporation (perhaps a suitable punishment for his involvement in the Nazi Party?) What would his diagnosis be? What would he say about 'being', 'death' and 'authenticity'? It is tempting to imagine Heidegger to surrender, maybe burst into tears, and declare: 'Today, it is not death – or *being-towards-death* which leads to authenticity. No, it is authenticity – this useless pursuit for the real and the different – which takes us to death.'

5

Failed Escapes

Now that work is no longer something we only *do*, but is also something we resolutely *are*, even infecting our DNA, the ways we try to escape it have become increasingly strange, evermore desperate. Watching a theatre of Italian mime artists, Paul Virilio finds that the once-captivating aspiration of adulthood (a mature, experienced, hardworking grown up with responsibilities) is now the very nightmare we want to escape. But how do we escape who we are? Virilio describes the scene, 'a dozen grown men wearing nappies and bibs and bustling around on stage, stumbling, fighting, falling, screaming, cuddling, playing ring o' roses, shutting each other out of the circle and so on ...' He continues, 'these burlesque figures were like neither children nor adults. They were false adults or false children – or perhaps caricatures of children. It was not easy to say precisely which.' What is perhaps certain is that these moments of symbolic regression or the desire to 'return' is indicative of how the new post-industrial militant glimpses utopia: not in the commune, not in the anarchist syndicate or even an extended leisurely holiday, but *in the nursery*.

Escaping what we are by refusing to accept our age isn't necessarily new. A defining trait of youth today is their refusal to be counted as a child – which ten-year-olds in push-up bras and high-heels unmistakably exemplify. But this is partly old news. For example, teenagers have always been reluctant to buy the magazines designed for their own age group. With their urge to be initiated into the exotic life of more experienced teenagers, gaining a preview of a life filled with dangerous sex, dating and fashion, they have routinely bought the magazines targeted for those older than themselves. But what about the reverse: grown ups buying children's magazines? It is this tragic form of escape we are more likely to witness today.

In *The Possibility of an Island*, Michel Houellebecq offers a useful example. The usually sad protagonist, Daniel, is seeing a woman who works for a newly established magazine, *Lolita*, named after Nabokov's famous novel. Realizing that the magazine she previously worked for, *20 Ans*, was not being bought by the twenty-year-olds it was originally produced for, but rather girls around fifteen or sixteen, one of the shareholders hit upon a brilliant business idea. With *Lolita* they would fill a new and previously undetected gap in the market. While officially being pitched to ten-year-olds, the magazine was in fact targeting their mothers. The shareholder had carefully thought it through:

> His bet was that, more and more, mothers would tend to copy their daughters. Obviously there's something ridiculous about a thirty-year-old woman buying a magazine called *Lolita*; but no more than her buying a clinging top, or hot-pants. His bet was that the feeling of ridiculousness, which had been so strong among women, and French women in particular, was going to gradually disappear and be replaced by pure fascination with limitless youth.

Youthfulness promises escape from the onerous and life-draining vagaries of adulthood. The modern corporation, too, has quite evidently discovered this secret yearning to become-child among its unhappy workforce. To this end it has invented all manner of games to replicate what it misperceives it is to be a child. These 'compulsory fun' techniques are no longer exclusively employed by the hip progressive IT firm, with a vision of the eternal youth, but can now be found even in the most unexpected places. *The New York Daily News* reported some years ago that the U.S. Postal

Service – a company that would only with great difficulty pass as a progressive symbol for the 'new economy' – had spent an enormous sum on team-building exercises, including activities where the employees had to wrap each other in toilet paper and aluminium foil, build sandcastles and imitate animals. In one of the more spectacular events, described as the climax of the 'annual recognition conference', the Postal Inspector General Karla Cocoran, was 'swaddled in a blue blanket and hoisted into the air above a hotel ballroom on colored ropes and strings manipulated by some 500 of her 725 employees'. And as a great finale to the same event, which was estimated to cost a total of $1.2 million, all of the participating postal service officers joined in singing the 1979 dance hit, 'We Are Family'.

These forays into infantilization represent the corporatization of what was from the beginning a pretty shaky method of escaping the living death of work. According to the *Living Scotsman*, the latest trend in workplace motivational techniques is 'inner child therapy', which 'aims to send us back in time, to an age when profit margins, deadlines and sales figures were stuff for mummy and daddy to worry about'. The comedian turned motivational therapist Gavin Oattes describes in the same article how he and his colleagues at the Tree of Knowledge like to do things differently: 'it's about rediscovering that inner child'. No one asks, of course, what happens if that inner child turns out to be pure evil, like little Isaac Chroner from *Children of the Corn*, unarguably the scariest movie of all time (only children can frighten us like that). Instead we find their weekly 'fun@work' workshop, advertised as a motivational event with a twist, where the participants are taken to the city's zoo – which in Oattes' opinion is the best place for reminding 'people of when they were a child'.

Of course, most workers realize all of this for what it is: ludicrous, stupid and oppressive. So why do we still take part? Perhaps *because we can*. Equipped with an infinitely reflexive consciousness, which functions as an oxygen tank in a world in which it is impossible to breathe, we are able to step forward with an air of indifference, not feeling a thing, completely numb. When Gavin Oattes and his colleagues take us to the zoo and involve us in game playing, we do not revolt with uncontrollable anger or disgust, but glide by with an inexplicable lightness. Our contempt may momentarily be revealed in feigned smiles and exaggerated nods. But our liberal education prevents us from passing inappropriate comments or offending those who seriously believe in it. The irony, of course, is that *no one* believes in it, perhaps least of all Gavin Oattes himself. His background as a comedian raises the suspicion that he is actually staging a wicked form of situational comedy, experimenting with the tragic lives of blank-eyed workers.

This begs an interesting question. Namely, what would happen if we refused to maintain this cynical distance? What if we were to take the words of these motivational therapists at face value and properly start behaving like children?

These are the questions that Polly Borland inadvertently touches on in her excellent book of photographs, *The Babies*. With an anthropological sensitivity, Borland documents the social and psychological world of a group of men, who like to call themselves 'adult babies'. Their desire is straightforward: they want to go back in time, to a state where they were still infants. Borland's pictures are set in what appears to be the babies' natural habitat: sitting in a giant crib in their homes, taking a ride in the pushchair down one of the local streets, dancing with like-minded friends in the backyard. Importantly, the images are not explained by any accompanying analytic texts. Nowhere does Borland succumb to the temptation to psychologize her subjects. Apart from name and place, we find no additional details that would help us figure these people out. Best of all, the sexual component is entirely passed over in silence. The focus is exclusively on the world they have created, a distinct world with its own particular rituals and systems of meaning. And it is precisely in this refusal to reduce her subjects to a set of pop-psychological categories ('unhappy childhood', 'denied breast-feeding', 'spoiled', 'beaten', etc.) that the power of the book resides. But also what makes it so provocative. Since how do we deal with this topic, in the absence of humour and scientific explanations?

Adult babies can only be discussed if first situated in the form of easily digestible humour or revulsion. One of the most popular characters from the BBC comedy show *Little Britain* is the forty-something Harvey, who routinely turns to his aging mother, asking for 'bitty'. Watching a grown up man sucking on his mother's breast, or having his diaper changed is the source of much amusement, at least on television. In real life, however, baby adults are suddenly no fun. As the obviously disgusted Christian Perring writes in one of the few available reviews of Borland's book: 'There is something profoundly strange in seeing grown men dress up in romper suits, sit in strollers, sucking on pacifiers, wearing large diapers, and silky nightdresses with pink bows. Without wishing to be needlessly judgmental, I have to say I find it far more grotesque than pictures of bondage gear and shiny leather'. He then continues, '"adult babies" are not evil, even if they are rather sad or pathetic'. This view is also expressed in endless comments on YouTube. Browsing through the comments to the few available clips about adult babies one is introduced to a world of unmitigated scorn, bolstered by a collo-quial hard-hitting style: 'this is just messed up, fucking freak', 'I would laugh, if it weren't so incredibly absurd', and more suggestive comments, like 'I found it very hard to masturbate to this'.

In the same vein, the rightwing Fox News commentator Neil Cavuto recently lamented the thirty-year-old adult baby, Stanley Thornton, who appeared in *National Geographic's* sensational (and in other respects very disappointing) documentary on the topic. When Cavuto discovered that Stanley received social security benefits, he lost his temper. In one of his most heated moments he rants: 'That thirty-year-old dude pretending to be a baby is nurtured on your dime. He collects social security from the crib. I'm not kidding you!'

So why this exaggerated anger? Adult babies certainly are resisting in a fairly strange manner the scam of adulthood, hijacked as it has been by the unbearable weight of the duty to work. But perhaps what really upsets the 'grown ups' is the way these adult babies reject the ideology of cynical distance – the real lynchpin of contemporary capitalism. It is not clear if the adult babies are being ironic. As much as irony is sanctioned in today's society – the stockbroker wearing a 'capitalism sucks' T-shirt, with the image of Vladimir Lenin giving the finger, is just hilarious – it nevertheless needs to be presented as unambiguously ironic, a criterion which the men in Borland's photographs fail to fulfil. Are they sincere? Can you be normal – having a job and kids and a car – and then at the same time enjoy being a baby?

What makes the adult babies so unsettling for people like Fox News' Neil Cavuto and the motivational therapist Gavin Oattes is that their mere presence conveys a truth that must not be uttered. With no signs of irony, they fully and openly play out the secret fantasy of becoming a child, of escaping work completely, which is exactly the same fantasy underlying team-building exercises, except expressed in a form not to be taken seriously. When we do so in such a public manner, like Borland's subjects, it immediately ruins the ideological bindings that tie us to the world of work.

The modern corporation too has discovered the joys of being an adult baby, but it can only function as capitalist ideology if it is couched in the language of irony ('we are not really babies') and consigned to the (openly) closeted under-life of the firm. A particularly telling example can be found in the California-based home security company, Alarm One. It was revealed that as part of their camaraderie building exercises, often used to kick-start another day of intense sales, they made their employees wear diapers, eat baby food, have pies thrown at them and were spanked in case they failed to meet the desired sales quota (crying was entirely at the discretion of workers). Such role-play was not an improvised aberration cooked up by some deranged sales manager. As reported by one of the salespersons, Janet Orlando, who was later to file a suit against Alarm One, some of the most senior people of the company, including the vice president, were active participants, making sure that everyone fulfilled their prescribed roles in the rite.

The game performed by Alarm One workers, effective only if it remains ironic and secret, is openly realized by Borland's adult babies, as an expression of their true, uncompromised, desire. It is tempting to recall Lacan's model of ethics as never compromising your desire. But we should be careful here. Note how one of Borland's subjects, Baby Cathy, describes his behavior in a related documentary:

> This is escapism. Escaping the real world. I'm leaving the real world behind, where all the bad things happen and everything is piling in. You're pressured, you need to meet deadlines. You got to do this, you got to do that. When I'm a baby, dressed like this, I'm outside the normal scope of life. I very quickly go into a mood of being a baby. I just relax. I find it very hard, after a while, to act like an adult.

Perhaps Baby Cathy is not compelled by the pure positive joy of being an infant (of which Lacan would perhaps approve), but by the negative push that everything non-infantile represents. In other words, this escape attempt ends up symbolically reinforcing (and perhaps even relies upon) the world of adults, the world of work. In Lacanian terms, this would have very little to do with ethics. Nevertheless, the desire to escape the real world – or more precisely, to momentarily exit the hyper-real world defined by capitalist realism – has become the default desire today. Cathy is here expressing the same lament as any other worn-out worker of post-industrialism.

But Baby Cathy's words could also be interpreted in a more orthodox Freudian sense. In the beginning of *Civilization and its Discontents*, Freud is struggling to come to terms with what one of his friends described as a religious experience, as 'a sensation of "eternity", a feeling as of something limitless, unbounded – as it were "oceanic"'. Unsurprisingly, Freud is less optimistic about the prospect of this 'oceanic feeling' than his friend, and confesses that he has never experienced such a sensation. Yet, he admits that he could possibly see it featuring in the early days of childhood, before the infant is introduced to civilization and the immense psychic suffering it entails: 'An infant at the breast does not as yet distinguish his ego from the external world as the source of the sensation flowing upon him.' Maybe Baby Cathy is merely seeking this experience of an oceanic feeling? The pacifier in his mouth reminds him of an existence where the ego and the external world was one. It is about returning to that moment, where existence was yet to make itself felt.

This desire – which Paul Valery has called 'the desire for the purity of non-being' – signals a more thoroughgoing wish to withdraw from the world, a world where classes in yoga, meditation, Feng Shui and Reiki represent a last vain attempt to assuaging our feeling of stress, offering us momentary flights from capitalist reality. And if this reality feels bereft of life, then strangely it is also *bereft of death*. As the simulation of life has given rise to entire industries, so too has the simulation of death. The stressed-out worker no longer seeks to escape the living death of work by imitating the sensuous pleasures of the living. No. Today, the only way to find relief is through mimicking death or that non-existence *before life*.

This probably explains the growing popularity of a special

club among the over-worked, hyper-stressed employees of London who simply cannot turn off. We, too, decided to visit this place. Located down a quiet backstreet in the inner city, a softly spoken young woman greeted us with a smile. We signed the indemnity forms and were gently escorted into a room. At the center, resembling alien pods, sat the flotation tanks. Consider the feeling. Effortlessly, your body floats in the super-saturated saltwater, and you realize that you can no longer distinguish between your different body parts. As you lie there, in the dark, hearing the ambient music slowly fading out, your brain activity slows down and you willingly surrender to a dream-like state. Then, finally, you have become no one.

Before the corporation discovered them, these tanks of death had an interesting history. In 1954, as part of his research on sensory deprivation, the then 39-year-old John C. Lily began his experiments on what would later become the floatation tank. Lily was his own test-pilot. He would lie there for hours, floating in the warm saltwater, devising new ways to improve the experience. The results were promising from the start. But it was not until he began to combine his floating with LSD that he was able to gain the sensation he ultimately desired: to completely evaporate. As he would later describe in an interview, 'I cried when I came back and found myself trapped in a body'. After his experiments with LSD, floating no longer appeared to Lily as depriving the senses. Rather it came to signify that moment of pure non-being, where the boundaries between self and other, body and mind, human and animal, life and death, were finally suspended. As the sociologist Johan Asplund writes in a brilliant essay: 'Lily was willing to die, again and again'.

Like sucking on a pacifier, descending yourself into the tank is a failed escape. Why? Because these practices will not set us apart from the world we try to escape. On the contrary, they tie us closer to the nightmare we wish to flee, allowing us to go back to work, to endure yet another soul-destroying day in the corporation. In other words, the brief illusory flight from capitalism only prolongs the suffering, as it makes us better prepared to go on, indefinitely, and more successfully. What might be called the 'escape industry' pitches itself as giving workers the chance to become more effective on the market. On the website of Floatworks, the world's largest flotation center, we find an entire section explaining how flotation therapy has a positive impact on our ability to work. Reportedly, we will not just become more relaxed, but also more creative: 'A float session is guaranteed to eliminate stress, leaving you with a clear mind to concentrate 100% on the matter in hand. It increases creativity, the ability to solve problems, concentration span, personal motivation and energy levels.'

There is a closely related avenue of escape available for the dead man working we have yet to consider: sickness. In his brilliant essay, 'Dreaming in Code', Rob Lucas writes:

> It is only when sickness comes and I am involuntarily rendered incapable of work that I really regain any extra time 'for myself'. It is a strange thing to rejoice at the onset of flu with the thought that, in the haze of convalescence, one may finally be able to catch up on things pushed aside by work. Here illness indeed appears as a 'weapon', but one that fights its own battle, not wielded by the supposed aggressor.

This is a complete inversion of the escape routes offered by European Buddhism, like yoga and meditation, and now 'flotation therapy'. Rather than responding to the persistent command to work by engaging in healthy alternatives, it is here suggested that the only vacation we can realistically hope for is provided through illness. When we have been officially declared sick, equipped with a recognized doctor's certificate, we are given a momentary break. For a second, we are left alone. As David Harvey observed, 'sickness is defined under capitalism broadly as inability to work'. Yes, we can breathe, but this rest does not last for long. Most sicknesses too soon come to an end. The sad truth is that although this strategy might allow for a momentary break, it still is, like the floatation tank and adult babies, defined more by what it is not (the tyranny of work) than by its own positive qualities. As Lucas concludes, 'if sickness is all we have, it offers little hope for meaningful resistance.'

* * *

It is no wonder that the flotation tank has become so popular. Like Lily, the dead man working is relentlessly looking for ways to momentarily escape a mode of life in which work is constantly present. We know the feeling all too well. We wait for the tsunami to wipe us away. But we fear it will never come. So in the meantime, we climb back into the pod. The music fades out. It is dark. We feel something. What is it? Is it … happiness? No. Not quite. It is just that momentary feeling of being left alone. A satisfactory feeling, no doubt, but one which will not last forever. When your sixty minutes of nothingness are over (and you are £40 poorer) you return again. And you cry. Just like John Lily did.

6

The Big Exit

With its magnificent rooftop garden overlooking central London, the French restaurant Coq d'Argent is, as a *Time Out* review has it, 'an obvious recommendation for people seeking a special-occasion venue'. Two days before his 25th birthday, on July 9, 2009, Anjool Malde, dressed in his favourite Hugo Boss suit, added a new twist to this description as he jumped off the eight-story roof with a glass of champagne in his hand. He was a stock-broker at Deutsche Bank. On the morning of his suicide, his employer had deleted his Bloomsbury account. He was also asked to leave early, not to interfere with an inquiry into an IT matter. No other details were made public. While his death was not the first in the series of banker suicides, it was arguably the most spectacular. 'He went out in style', as his family is reported to have said.

Almost one year earlier, in late September 2008, the 47-year-old Kirk Stephenson jumped in front of a 100 mph express train, thus marking the start of what was later to be described as a banker's suicide epidemic. As a chief operating officer at the Chelsea-based Olivant Advisors Ltd., Stephenson made £330,000 a year. In a statement, later read to the jury at Buckinghamshire Coroner's Court, his wife wrote:

'When the banking system started to collapse, he became very tense and worried about a lot of things he had worked hard for. He was slowly getting more worried and on Monday, 22 September, he came home for dinner. He looked very stressed and mentioned killing himself over the credit crunch but he could not do it because he loved me and the child too much.'

Apart from his wife, Stephenson left behind an eight-year-old son.

On December 17 the same year, the Danish-born Christen Schnor, HSBC's head of insurance for the UK, Turkey, the Middle East and Malta, was found dead on Jumeriah Carlton Tower Hotel in Knightsbridge. He had hanged himself with his own belt. According to a Metropolitan Police spokesman, he 'was pronounced dead at the scene'. The motive was not established, although *The Daily Telegraph* pointed to 'serious problems in his marriage'. Another daily newspaper reported that Schnor had regularly gone missing from his work, 'as he embarked on a personal journey of destruction'. A source speaking to the newspaper said that he had 'been spending a small fortune booking prostitutes through an escort agency and buying drugs'. Schnor left behind two children and a wife.

Colin Birch committed suicide by hanging on July 30, 2010. He had recently lost his job as assistant vice president at Deutsche Bank. He was found dead by two prostitutes who unknowingly had been paid to assist his suicide. They had met him in the forest of Dartford Heath, in Kent, just after midnight. On their arrival, they found Birch crying. He was standing on a chair, with a noose around his neck. They were instructed to verbally abuse him, saying he 'deserved to die'. As they were later to say in the following interrogations, Birch had told them that he was wearing a safety harness, and that it was all about a sadomasochistic performance. Their story was supported by a text message sent by Birch to the escort service prior to the meeting:

Girl will ask for execution fee and I will go to place of execution.
My crime is being a looser.
Girl kicks away stool and laughs then walks back to car without looking back to show she has no feelings.

After having verbally abused Birch, the two prostitutes left the scene for a short while. As they returned, Birch's lips had turned blue. He was no longer breathing. They were paid £60 each.

Exactly how many suicides followed in the wake of the financial meltdown is unclear. There are no statistics to be trusted. And many have pointed out that the real suicide wave is yet to arrive, since it is usually not until a number of years after the crisis, when the effects have made themselves felt more forcefully, that the real tragedy kicks in.

Either way, these suicides are unmistakably tragic, in the literal sense of the word. Jumping off a roof with a glass of champagne in your hand produces a dazzling, almost mythic image. However, it is arguably not in tragedy that we find the answer to these suicides, but in 18th century England. In his essay on suicide weapons, Ian Hacking observes that the defining aristocratic vices during this period were 'duelling, suicide, and gambling'. In this light, the recent wave of suicides could be read as the final achievement of the bankers, transforming them into a postmodern version of the aristocrat. Gambling rather explains itself. Carelessly playing with large stakes without seriously considering the consequences is a description of banking few would object to, least of all bankers themselves. Duelling doesn't seem equally apparent, at least not if we think about it in the more traditional sense of the word. However, a recent article in *The Huffington Post* has described the emergence of what they call 'Wall Street Fight Clubs'. With inspiration from the movie (and novel) of the same name, bankers now meet after work to beat each other up. Unlike the duelling of the eighteenth century, which would typically take place at a beautiful location, under ceremonial circumstance with elegant outfits, the bankers meet half-naked in basement gyms. Partly an underground phenomenon, it has nevertheless attained a widespread acceptance. Even the chief executive officer of Deutsche Bank Securities is reported to give his support, saying 'it's a great stress reliever'. The aristocracy of the 18th century, of course, dabbled with duelling, suicide and gambling to escape a deep-seated feeling of boredom. Bankers, on the other hand, are not bored. That would be a blessing. No, they seek to escape their living death by flirting with the real thing, since only risky behaviour allows a glimpse of some kind of conclusion.

On the other side of the income spectrum we find what might be called working class suicide. Inside the heavily secured complex outside Shenzhen, China, known as the Foxconn City, we find the home of about 420,000 workers. Apart from being the world's largest producer of electronic gadgetry, assembling a range of Apple's products, Foxconn is perhaps most famous for the recent string of suicides, inaugurated by the 25-year-old Sun Danyong as he jumped from his dormitory window in 2009. On the surface, Foxconn does not look like a labor camp. A guided tour through the premises yields a picture quite unlike the factories of the industrial dark ages. Here we find swimming pools, tennis courts and gyms as well as numerous clubs for employees, in chess, calligraphy and fishing, to name a few. The only catch is that none of these facilities are to be used. Apart from short breaks for lunch and sleep, the workers have no free time. The swimming pools and tennis courts appear therefore to be cruel props, designed to give the impression that an end to work might come. But like our menacing tsunami, it never does.

To investigate the working conditions at Foxconn, the Chinese newspaper *Southern Quarterly* sent a team of undercover reporters. After 28 days of immense suffering they came back to report about a life completely overtaken by work. As they reported: 'The workers we have spoken to say that their hands continue to twitch at night, or that when they are walking down the street they cannot help but mimic the motion. They are never able to relax their minds'. As one of the reporters surmised, 'for many workers, the only escape from this cycle was to end their life'. In the attempt to curb the suicide epidemic, Foxconn management have gone to great lengths. They have put safety nets between buildings to catch falling workers. They have opened a stress room, where employees can beat up life-sized dolls with baseball bats. Over a hundred counsellors have been called in. And thirty Buddhist monks have been summoned, 'to release the suicide souls from purgatory'. Foxconn are now leading innovators in a new field of management ... suicide management.

Somewhere between the spectacular suicides in the financial sector and the Chinese working class flinging themselves off factory roofs, is France Télécom. Some figures suggest that over sixty employees have committed suicide. Senior management has shrugged off criticism by pointing to the national suicide rate, which is just marginally lower than that found in France Télécom. The fact remains, however, that the majority of the suicides were explicitly linked to dissatisfaction with the restructuring of the firm. Since France Télécom became privatized in 1998, some 40,000 jobs have disappeared, and the remaining workers have been facing harsher conditions, with more stress, more management, more work.

While the lifestyles of these three groups widely vary, they all have something in common: the preference for death over a non-life of work. Just as the Foxconn employee who involuntarily continues to mimic the motion from the factory line in his bed, the banker is just as likely to dream within the logic of the stock market, with random flashing figures interrupting the silence of the night. As their lives slowly disappear, death is suddenly nothing to be afraid of. It becomes a gift; an option that carries a certain lightness. The dead man working, in this sense, is similar to the anonymous victim in James Cameron's film *Aliens*. The doomed heroes discover the young woman encased in alien-slime, being used to incubate and hatch terrible creatures. Presuming she is dead, we are horrified when she opens her eyes, quietly begging: 'please kill me ... please kill me!' She demands a second death, a real death. Similarly, we can imagine the stockbroker on the underground late at night, silently humming a tune playing on his iPod: 'suicide is painless'.

A life neither distinguishable from the deadness of work nor the lightness of death is a life not worth living. To understand this, it is essential to return to David Hume's great essay on suicide, which, because of its apparent blasphemy, could only be published after his death. For Hume, we have no obligation to our Creator, to God, to prolong our existence unless it contains at least a modicum of meaning and pleasure. Indeed, in the face of immense and unending pointlessness, we no longer have a duty to go on: 'why may I not cut short these miseries at once by an action which is no more prejudicial to society?' Hume, finally, adds: 'The power of committing suicide is regarded by Pliny as an advantage which men posses even above the Deity himself'. In other words, 'suicide is man's way of telling God, "You can't fire me – I quit"', as the American comedian Bill Maher has put it.

Hume's thoughts on suicide outraged his public when finally published, but they have made him immensely popular today, not least among euthanasia supporters. With reference to Hume, among others, these interest groups insist on the right to terminate one's own life, at least when it has come to a point when we decide it is no longer considered worth living. The troubling question arising here is whether we could determine a set of 'objective' or 'external' circumstances, so grave in character, that they would legitimate suicide. It is tempting to predict that if such objective criteria were found, then most corporations today would need their own suicide squads, rather large in size, to assist the thousands of workers who would be queuing for death.

Cioran, in stark contrast, claims that 'no one commits suicide for external reasons, only because of inner disequilibrium'. For him, there are no rational incentives for committing suicide, 'only organic, secret causes which predetermine it'. In short, suicide is a strictly private affair.

After the suicide scandal broke out, France Télécom's management made a public announcement in which they declared that the deaths were prompted by personal, not professional, causes, thus reflecting Cioran's view that suicide is dispositional rather than situational. What this fails to take into account, however, is the fact that the post-industrial condition has shattered the boundary between the professional and the personal. As we have demonstrated in the previous chapters, the logic of work is now intimately enmeshed in who we are, regulating even the most elementary functions of life. We have become our jobs, and therefore an obvious way to end the tyranny of work might be to end ourselves.

Against this background it is interesting to consider the occupation with the highest suicide rate. And no, it is not the banker, the clerk or the factory worker who is most likely to check out early. It is the artist. 'Hardly surprising', some would sigh, thus rehearsing the ingrained assumption that artists have always been lonely and self-destructive souls. Just look at Rembrandt, Rothko, Sylvia Plath, Ian Curtis – they were all melancholic brooders. Such dispositional explanations, however common they might be, not only betray rather silly bourgeois values; they also overlook the structural conditions under which artists commonly work and live: constant stress, self-employment, flexible working hours, no regulating contract and income, no pension scheme and low pay. In other words conditions almost identical to those now spreading through the post-industrial landscape. While the nature of the job is probably devoid of anything creative other than ways to avoid it, the material conditions of many employees today are increasingly mirroring the precarity of the artist.

In her recent essay 'When Life Goes to Work', Isabelle Graw deepens this connection between the artist and the post-industrial employee by demonstrating how Andy Warhol would now be considered the ideal worker. The flamboyant wig-wearing pop-artist is every progressive manager's wet dream. He is anti-conformist, socially skilled, and immensely creative. But more importantly, he displays a particular attitude towards work and life, one where the two are almost indistinguishable. Warhol hated relaxation as much as he hated vacations. 'Even having fun meant working, since he used every social occasion (such as parties) in order to "get more portraits" or "more ideas" or to "sell more ads for *Interview*"'. In this sense, Warhol could be said to fully realize the injunctions placed upon us today via biopolitics and extreme neoliberalism. In an agile manner, he absorbed and met all those pressures that now bombard not just the artist but everyone living under the spell of 'the new spirit of capitalism'. For Graw this is 'the pressure to use and, inevitably, instrumentalize your friendships; the pressure to communicate, to produce and glean information; the pressure to show up in person and to be present; the pressure to perform convincingly; the pressure to look good, to stay fit, to be one's own product, to sell oneself, and to market one's own life'.

Graw points out that the content of Warhol's work is guided by the question of death, particularly with regard to celebrity, crisis and mourning. However, she fails to see how Warhol's work ethic itself was also underpinned by the shadow of death, especially after he was gunned down, and seriously wounded, by the feminist writer Valerie Solanas. After he was shot, Warhol said:

Before I was shot, I always thought that I was more half-there than all-there – I always suspected that I was watching TV instead of living life. Right when I was being shot and ever since, I knew that I was watching television.

Warhol continues:

The doctors and everyone else, including me, was sure I was going to die, so we all got ready, and then I didn't do it. But I always wished I had died, and I still wish that, because I could have gotten the whole thing over with.

Warhol clearly feared death and thought it better to get it out of the way. But an alternative reading can be made when considering his well known desire to become a machine. As he famously stated: 'Machines have less problems. I'd like to be a machine, wouldn't you?' Here, we could perhaps see his desire for death as the desire to slowly become an inanimate object, one which would not need to face the terror of a living death, because it has already inhabited the space of the non-living. In this respect, Warhol embodies a particularly acute symptom of life under late capitalism today: a living death, overwhelmingly governed by the principles of work.

Like Warhol, the dead man working hates vacations, mainly because a break from work would immediately remind him what life has otherwise become. But is he suicidal? Can the dead man working take his own life? Probably not. After all, if one is already declared dead, it makes little sense to kill oneself. As the indie pop band Bad Cash Quartet sing in what could easily be the soundtrack to the dead man working, 'I am much too bored to die'. Life is boring, but so, too, is death. This comes very close to what Cioran concluded. Rhetorically asking himself why he didn't commit suicide, he says: 'because I am as sick of death as I am of life.'

'The thought of suicide is a powerful solace', Nietzsche once famously said, 'by means of it one gets through many a bad night'. Suicide for the dead man working hence exists as a reassuring option, at times appealing, but for the most part superfluous, because death has already arrived in a more profound, more inescapable form. When one of the author's colleagues recently retired, he said that he sometimes dreamt of dying in a meeting, 'because the transition from life to death would be absolutely minimal'.

Compared to this prolonged living death of the contemporary worker, the string of suicides described at the beginning of this chapter suddenly looks less tragic. The humiliating double-bind facing the dead man working is this: if they cannot live, then neither can they die. Therein lies the true tragedy – a fate worse than death. As a junior management consultant told one of the authors: 'I realized things were bad whenever I boarded a plane for work, I always prayed it would crash.' Only in the hope of an externally imposed and catastrophic death does freedom become discernible. Perhaps, then, we should revive the classical motto of 'learning how to die'. By educating ourselves in the difficult art of dying we might achieve something above and beyond the sentence of protraction. As Hervé Jurvin puts it in his book *The Coming of the Body*: 'What is left to die of a body from which all life – all pleasure, all projects, all relationships – has withdrawn?' The paradox here is that we ironically need to affirm life in order to end it successfully. Otherwise death becomes just another puerile exit fantasy. When discussing this disappearance of death from the horizon of human life, Jurvin claims that the only thing the human individual has left, to save his integrity, is 'to make his death the final act of a life lived in freedom'.

So is it possible, or even desirable, to imagine suicide as a successful exit? Here, we do well to reconsider the economist Albert O. Hirschman's classic essay on the three key responses to the corporation: 'loyalty' (we remain truthful to the enterprise and internalize its commands), 'voice' (we protest the injustices of work by making our voices heard) and 'exit' (we simply withdraw from the relationship altogether). Of course, all of these responses are now untenable. Loyalty is outrageous. And protest, as we have seen, merely puts us on the radar for the next wave of downsizing, or even worse, identifies us as a prime candidate for the next round of promotions. Exit, finally, is marginally more tenable. The problem is where do we go? Now, for all intents and purposes *we are the corporation*. And how do you escape yourself?

We might yield more interesting results if we read each response to the corporation through the very lens of taking your own life. It is through this reading that Hirschman's typology really comes into its own and begins to makes sense. To help us, let's superimpose it onto Žižek's three modes of suicide. The first type, which would correspond to loyalty, is the *passage à l'acte*. No reason is normally given (there are no notes or prior unsuccessful attempts as a cry for help). It seems to come from nowhere, and is shocking because it signifies only itself. There is no distance between the suicide's identity and the failed object that has slowly become their life (work, the stock market, the bank account). This is an act that remains loyal to the command that has already defined us. For example, the banker who ends his life when the economy dips is conveying a complete identification with the market and the failing firm, and finds that this is obviously the most logical thing to do. We could also say that the very first suicide at Foxconn, performed by Sun Danyong (before the less original copycat deaths), could be seen in a similar light. Rather than creating distance between the killing conditions of factory work – perhaps dreaming that one day they might swim in the pool – they remain true to the command, and become what they know the company secretly desires them to be: dead. This is the ultimate form of loyalty to the firm, and for that reason, a failure.

The second kind of suicide aims to convey a message, to 'voice' the reasons why one has decided to die. Take, for example, the suicides at France Télécom. Numerous suicide notes were left behind, declaring that they could no longer go on because they had been ruined by their jobs. In this type of suicide the Other is addressed directly, usually with text or methods of termination that are horrendously graphic – one French Télécom employee made his point in no uncertain terms by setting himself on fire. We must, of course, consider this type of suicide a failure too. It is propelled by the imagined effect on an audience *following* the discovery of the body. It assumes we can be present at our own funeral. But there is no afterwards, only black nothingness. This makes it a wasted death, a gift to an undeserving Other who in the end doesn't even care.

It is only really the last type of suicide, corresponding to exit, which comes close to what we might describe as a 'successful act' – if at all there is such a thing. According to Žižek, this symbolic suicide involves:

> [T]he erasure of the symbolic network that defines the subject's identity, of cutting off all the links that anchor the subject in its symbolic substance. Here, the subject finds itself totally deprived of its symbolic identity, thrown into the 'night of the world' in which its only correlative is the minimal of an excremental leftover, a piece of trash, a mote of dust in the eye, an almost-nothing that sustains the pure Place-Frame-Void, so that here, finally, 'nothing but the place takes place'.

This kind of suicide is not loyal to the corporation. Neither is it a voice that inadvertently gifts the death to an Other who despises us. It is a more complete and uncompromising withdrawal from any discursive relation with the world of work. If capital and life have become indistinguishable, then how could we know, taste or feel the latter? This is precisely what the symbolic suicide aims to achieve, to rethink life from the perspective of death. It is only by killing ourselves, as we know it, that we could start anew. For this reason, it is not enough to kill the boss or set the corporation on fire. Because, ultimately, we *are* the boss; we are the embodiment of the corporation. To kill ourselves, symbolically, is to kill the boss function. In classic Freudian terms, suicide is the killing of that hated other, which you have internalized so perfectly that you cannot distinguish it from your own sense of self. That unwanted other is the boss, it is the *you* that needs to be put to sleep if you ever want to live again.

Montaigne writes that 'learning how to die is to unlearn how to be a slave'. But to unlearn how to be a slave also means that we need to unlearn how to live. In an ironic way, we know everything about life. We have read all about it in innumerable magazines and books. We have memorized the checklists for what objectively passes as the good life. We have learnt it as schoolchildren learn mathematics, superficially, well enough to pass the exams, but without even trying to go beyond the repetitive functions we have programmed into ourselves. Unlearning life, then, is what the symbolic suicide attempts to achieve, to wipe out ourselves in a way that re-creates a new vista.

* * *

Night has fallen for the last time. You lie awake and listen to the dead silence surrounding you. That's when you hear it. It is still far away, but you are not mistaken. You have waited long enough now. It is dark. You cannot even see your own body. It draws closer. Finally. No more early morning meetings. No more emails. The wave is here. It wipes you away.

Postscript: What Does a Little Girl Want?

It is no surprise that when capitalism was declared dead in the late 1970s, yet paradoxically became the only game in town – epitomized by the rise of neoliberalism – it was the *child* who emerged as the preeminent figure of emancipatory hope. For sure, the child has always been good for this role. We need look no further than Rimbaud's wolf-children of the Paris Commune or the inscrutable revolutionary moment of Joan of Arc. It is only today, however, when the working adult has become a wrecked and unsalvageable project, that the child figure truly assumes a formidable counter-force. If working today means being unable to distinguish oneself from one's job; and one's identities and desires from the cold logic of the market, it's the child's uncanny ability to escape this co-presence that deserves serious attention. Unlike the dead man working, the child is neither depressed nor caught in a circle of bizarre escape attempts. The child is merely on strike. Indeed, it's not the usual worker's strike we encounter here, but a strike that goes to the bottom of who we are, a *human strike*. When there is no clear separation between *what we do* and *who we are* – the great tragedy of the post-industrial condition – we have to extend the meaning of the strike to include our very person. The refusal of going to work only makes sense if we also refuse what work has made us become. It is here that we need to consider the child. Because only the child can provide the expertise to escape the straitjacket of 'being human' (or what has come to pass for this after years of corporatization). But what kind of child? A *little boy* or a *little girl*? The difference is crucial.

In the early 1980s two films, both based on Stephen King novels, unwittingly answered this question. Perhaps inspired by the coming wave of neoliberalism, *The Shining* and *Fire Starter* cast children in the role of the revolutionary subject. In *The Shining*, seven-year-old Danny is gifted with 'the shine', a curious ability to see the murdered ghosts crowding the deserted hotel, which his mother and father are looking after over a cold, dark winter. It is not far-fetched to see the hotel as a representation of a hostile market society that appears inescapable, a playground for the living dead exemplified by the ever-growing madness of Jack Torrance (played by Jack Nicholson). In the end, however, the boy manages to escape by outwitting his now insane father, losing him in a garden maze, where he freezes to death. The child has spoken.

In *Fire Starter* it is the young girl Charlie, played by Drew Barrymore, who is cast as the hero. Before she was born, her parents were made subjects to some rather unusual experiments by a secret branch of the CIA, The Shop. As a result Charlie was born with extremely powerful pyrotechnic abilities. Anyone messing with her would immediately be set on fire. Her sense of justice is keen, however. In the beginning of the film she overhears a young soldier at the airport telling his pregnant lover that he no longer wants her. Charlie sets his feet on fire. ('Do you mind if I put my feet out first?' he asks the cop demanding him to get out of the toilet bowl.) Of course, the military had plans to put these abilities to their use too, so after her mother is killed, Charlie and her father go on the run.

The Shop and its murderous secret agents clearly represent a pernicious state capitalism that aims to transform everyday people into weapons of mass destruction. And we should note that it is no coincidence that the agency, which could be read as neoliberalism's desire to commodify every facet of human life, even a little girl's thoughts and feelings, is called The Shop. By the end of the film, the agents capture and kill her father. In retaliation, Charlie unleashes a devastating wall of fire, setting ablaze all the wrongdoers, melting their bullets and utterly destroying the whole compound. Once again, the child has spoken.

Both films cleverly reverse the adult-kid roles to demonstrate the revolutionary abilities of the child-figure. In *The Shining* it is the parents who behave like petulant children – Jack even rehearses a nursery rhyme as he pursues his terrified son with an axe. In *Fire Starter*, it's Charlie who cares for her ailing father, comforting him as he becomes weaker and more enfeebled. But Danny and Charlie are neither children nor adults, but something else, making them inscrutable, and so, difficult to read. They seem to break with a politics of recognition that might have otherwise lured them onto the stage of power, thus forcing them to speak using its words, its terminology and its expectations. As a number of thinkers including Nietzsche remind us, only kids can ignore power and thus reformat themselves in this fashion. It is this child-like ability to *become invisible* that is useful when thinking about how to escape bio-capitalism. As the logic of the market and the corporation become universal, complete, to resist means finding an escape route, a method of exit, abandoning an unsalvageable world. This involves detaching oneself and social relations from the logic of work, which otherwise continues to haunt us, spilling over into our memories, feelings, habits and worries. In this sense, Hardt and Negri nicely put it thus, 'don't try to save yourself – in fact, your self has to be sacrificed!'

However, the children in the two films do this in very different ways. In *The Shining* Danny fights by assimilating the code of power, identifying with the ghosts to such an extent that they begin to inhabit his world and him theirs. He fights by keeping his enemies close. The central motif here is *paranoia*. They are everywhere, overcrowding the boy's poor little head. And he wants them gone, something which can be achieved only by outsmarting them at their own game. This is also what makes Danny's resistance risky. It isn't too far from a reactionary attachment to the very thing that we are endeavouring to escape. Little boys don't work so well here.

Charlie on the other hand is different. We don't really learn much about her internal state of mind or her feelings (it must be said here that Drew Barrymore's exceptionally bad acting helps convey this vacant state). She escapes in precisely the opposite way to Danny, not by welcoming the enemy into her own world, but by a massive evacuation of the human, leaving only an indefinable instantiation of the body. This is what terrified the authorities so much, since they had no way to capture her, no way to communicate with her, which never became more obvious than when she opened her mouth to speak.

The little girl represents a withdrawal from power. But becoming a little girl is no easy task. Even to imagine withdrawing – which, for the little girl, seems to come so easily – is a hard thing to do, especially when power is so close to us, so insidious. The subject of power remains paralyzed, unable to act. To illustrate this paralysis we have to look no further than to our 'sleep worker', Rob Lucas, whose dreams had even become a place of work, and for whom exit was nowhere to be seen. He writes,

> given the individually allocated and project centered character of the job, absenteeism only amounts to self-punishment, as work that is not done will have to be done later under increased stress. Given the collaborative nature of the work, heel dragging necessarily involves a sense of guilt towards other workers. On the production line, sabotage might be a rational tactic, but when your work resembles that of an artisan, sabotage would only make life harder.

All the motifs of self-entrapment are here. Of course, Lucas could easily resist his work. Just not in the manner that characterizes traditional forms of protest. And this is difficult to see since *how does one resist what appears to be life itself?* We think it involves a process of *de-working* our bodies and social relations, separating life from that which has now colonized it. This means not mistaking the commonwealth that we produce together for capitalism. Not mistaking life and its conduct for work. Not mistaking the body and its sensibilities for a human resource. Not mistaking self-direction and its improvisational energies for the injunction to work or the boss function. Each mistaken conflation creates conditions ripe for self-entrapment – the true currency of biocracy. Each detachment, however, represents a positive moment of removal, separation, or withdrawal from the scene of power. A return to the rich and life-affirming flows of social living that is so anathema to existence under capitalism.

This is the bigger exit, more particularly the suicide, and more particularly still the symbolic suicide, which cuts ourselves loose from the symbolic network. This exit involves leaving a dying world behind, with no feelings of regret or nostalgia. Let's put on some Morrissey:

Say farewell to your fairweathered friends
And not a second too soon
To leave a life among ruins
Well there was nothing left but to
Cut ourselves loose
These fascists and philistines
Of violence and fashion
These modern day philistines
They stand on your hands
They stand on my hands
Any day now we'll perish
These are nervous times

But what prevents us from walking out on our 'fairweathered friends' is the belief that we can continue going on like this, in a barely tolerable life. Consider the dead man working, standing arrested and debilitated before the wave – the ultimate figure of self-entrapment. He can neither live nor die. But a small modification, a quick and precise cut, is perhaps all that is required to overcome this impasse.

The difficult art of walking away from a parasitical world of work is no better explored than in Deleuze and Guattari's *A Thousand Plateaus*, perhaps the handbook for resisting the kind of power we now have to confront, a power that comes in the guise of an intimate yet fascist, philistine, and fairweathered friend. They argue that the little girl, strangely enough, represents a way out. They take this from Nietzsche who said we must move from the camel who carries too much, to the lion who fights too much, to the child who simply lets go and starts to live again on its own terms. Or more precisely, the angry, indolent female child. Only little girls truly understand that there is nothing more incapacitating and terrible today than being a human (resource). They see it for what it is, a blockage manufactured only to work and then die without fuss. Whereas the little boy is often too neurotic and paranoid to let go – Danny was always worrying about something – the little girl makes her unfathomable qualities her prime weapon. She resists being read, she forgets, and remains unmarred by an overbearing conscience. And like Charlie in *Fire Starter* she represents a pure and inscrutable externalization. There is nothing inside for biocracy to attach itself to. And as the agents for The Shop in *Fire Starter* discovered, you don't want to piss her off. We doubt Deleuze and Guattari had the chance to read King's *Fire Starter* by the time *A Thousand Plateaus* was published (in 1980 in French). But if they did, perhaps they would have found their revolutionary subject. They write:

> Girls do not belong to an age group, sex, order, or kingdom: they slip in everywhere, between orders, acts, ages, sexes … Trost, a mysterious author, painted a portrait of the girl, to whom he linked the fate of the revolution: her speed, her freely machinic body, her intensities, her abstract line of flight, her indifference to memory, her non-figurative character. The special role of the girl in Russian terrorism: the girl with the

bomb, the guardian of dynamite?

The little girl is not defined by biological age. Its figure is open to anyone of all ages, even the dead man working. And they like to roam, a perpetual escape into life. Whereas the oppressive and hermetically sealed hotel in *The Shining* is a defining signature of the film, what we notice when watching *Fire Starter* is how Charlie is always on the move (often persuading her father to carry her – little girls are always lazy, clearly an admirable quality in a society obsessed with work). Indeed, Charlie is one of the most nomadic characters in cinema. And when she finally does get imprisoned by The Shop, she quickly burns the place down. Deleuze and Guattari suggest that becoming-little-girl is defined by a politics of *imperceptibility*. As they elaborate, 'movement is the essential relation to the imperceptible … and movement, like the girl as a fugitive being, cannot be perceived.' Charlie's father reminds her what she already knows: 'we've got to keep moving, in single-file, like Indians, and keep as far to the edge of the road as possible.' Keep moving and stay out of sight.

* * *

'What does a woman want?', was the one question Freud could never resolve. It continued haunting him to the last days of his life. Today, as the streets of London are still smoldering, the truly unsettling question is: 'what does a little girl want'?

Acknowledgment

We are grateful to Casper Hoedemeakers, Michael Marinetto and André Spicer for having read and commented on previous drafts of this book.

Contemporary culture has eliminated both the concept of the public and the figure of the intellectual. Former public spaces – both physical and cultural – are now either derelict or colonized by advertising. A cretinous anti-intellectualism presides, cheerled by expensively educated hacks in the pay of multinational corporations who reassure their bored readers that there is no need to rouse themselves from their interpassive stupor. The informal censorship internalized and propagated by the cultural workers of late capitalism generates a banal conformity that the propaganda chiefs of Stalinism could only ever have dreamt of imposing. Zer0 Books knows that another kind of discourse – intellectual without being academic, popular without being populist – is not only possible: it is already flourishing, in the regions beyond the striplit malls of so-called mass media and the neurotically bureaucratic halls of the academy. Zer0 is committed to the idea of publishing as a making public of the intellectual. It is convinced that in the unthinking, blandly consensual culture in which we live, critical and engaged theoretical reflection is more important than ever before.